TAIN THROUGH THE CENTURIES

TAIN THROUGH THE CENTURIES

R. W. MUNRO AND JEAN MUNRO

Birlinn

*This reprint has been funded by Highland Council Ross &
Cromarty Area Committee, mainly from the Tain Common
Good Fund augmented by a contribution from Councillor
Alasdair Rhind's own area discretionary budget allocation*

This edition published in 2005 by
Birlinn Limited
West Newington House
10 Newington Road
Edinburgh
EH9 1QS

www.birlinn.co.uk

First published in 1966

British Library Cataloguing in Publication Data
A catalogue record for this book is available from
the British Library

ISBN10: 1 84158 338 3
ISBN13: 978 1 84158 338 9

Printed and bound by Antony Rowe Ltd, Chippenham

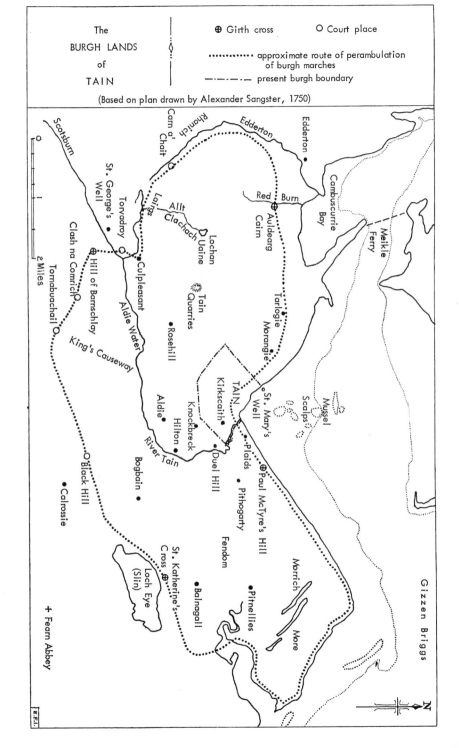

The
BURGH LANDS
of
TAIN

⊕ Girth cross   O Court place

•••••••• approximate route of perambulation
of burgh marches

—·—·— present burgh boundary

(Based on plan drawn by Alexander Sangster, 1750)

Scotsburn
Cam a' Chait
Rhenich
Edderton
Edderton

St. George's Well
Tonvdroy
Largs
Allt Clachach
Lochan Uaine
Red Burn
Auldearg Cairn
Cambuscurrie Bay
Meikle Ferry

Clash na Comrich
Hill of Barnschlay
Culpleasant
Aldie Water
Tain Quarries
Tarlogie
Morangie

Tornabuachail
King's Causeway
Rosehill
Kirkscaith
TAIN
St. Mary's Well
Scalps
Mussel

Aldie
Hilton
Knockbreck
Duel Hill
Plaids
Paul McTyre's Hill

Bogbain
River Tain
Pithogarty
Morrich More

Black Hill
Fendom
Gizzen Briggs

Calrossie
Loch Eye (Slin)
St. Katherine's Cross
Balnagall
Pitnellies

+ Fearn Abbey

N

Z.F.I.

Preface to the Birlinn Edition

THE time has come, indeed is long overdue, for a reprint of the official history of Tain commissioned and published by Tain Town Council in 1966. It has been out of print for many years now. Much has happened in the intervening thirty-eight years including, sadly, the passing of one of the co-authors, R. W. Munro. When the prospect of a reprint, considered as a possibility for several years, finally became a reality, the intention was to add a chapter to bring Tain's story up to date. However, we have come to the conclusion that this is not the place to do this and the book should remain as it stands. Instead, we propose to provide only a brief summary of some of the major changes.

Who would have thought, certainly not Tain Councillors as they embarked on their Ninth Centenary Celebrations, that less than a decade later Town Councils would cease to exist? Nonetheless, 1975 saw local government changes introduced which resulted in their demise, and with them their proud traditions, to be replaced by District Councils then Community Councils with most of the power and authority being invested in the regional bodies. The main result of this being that Tain, like other communities, lost much of the control of its affairs.

Many other things have come, and sometimes gone. The new Tain Royal Academy finally opened in 1969. After a campaign to ensure its preservation, the old academy building was converted into a residential home for the elderly, Duthac House. Now thirty-plus years on it is threatened with closure. An aluminium smelter came to Easter Ross in 1971 (sited near the deep-water facility of the Cromarty Firth). Barely a decade later, it ceased production and still lies empty, stripped of its assets, though at the time of writing, it has been proposed as a possible location of a large pulp and wood processing plant. The 1970s also saw the development of North Sea Oil. Among other oil-related developments it brought to the area was an oil-rig building yard at Nigg. It reached its heyday in the mid 1970s and since then its fortunes have fluctuated, never again reaching those dizzy heights. It has had to seek other lines to remain in existence at all. The latest bid is to construct aircraft carriers. These two developments caused a boom and bust situation which affected Tain as well as the other Easter Ross communities. Tain businesses and services received a boost and the town expanded, then it suffered along with their decline.

Significant developments in communications — the building of Tain by-pass and bridges over each of the three firths, Beauly, Cromarty and Dornoch — have also made an impact. Tain has possibly gained to some extent from the improved link to the north but this has been more than offset by the shortening of the journey to Inverness.

Some things still remain. The Mussel Scalps still play an important part providing funds to help finance improvements, albeit that use of the Common Good is now subject to approval of the regional body. Glenmorangie Distillery, recently in the hands of new owners, is still thriving and attracts many visitors each year. Tain can still offer many services and facilities. Tain Golf Club has emerged from the shadow of Royal Dornoch GC (popularised by Tom Watson and other American golfers) as many more golfers are pleasantly surprised when they 'discover' it for the first time and spread the word. Tain Tennis Club has experienced a marked revival over recent years. The old blaes courts have been replaced by all weather courts and a new pavilion will soon follow. Football and bowling are still catered for.

In more recent times, the formation of a Tain Initiative Group, the appointment of a Projects Officer, co-operation between communities through a Small Towns Network group, various other initiatives and the efforts of volunteer groups to make the town more attractive to businesses and visitors, are all helping to regenerate the town and restore some local pride. Thus, although it no longer can offer the range of shops and services it once did, Tain has acquired a number of new facilities. Tain Royal Academy Community Complex (TRACC), adjacent to and operating in conjunction with the Academy, and the Duthac Centre (formerly the Town Hall and even earlier the Parish Church) between them offer a range of leisure, recreational and social facilities, including a games hall and swimming pool. In the last year or two, part of the Academy playing fields has been developed as an all-weather floodlit facility and a skateboard park, along with the conversion of the old boating pond into a wildlife pond, have further enhanced the open space facilities on The Links. The wildlife pond compliments an existing Environmental Garden developed from a piece of waste ground in the early 1990s. A number of years ago Tain acquired an excellent Youth Café which continues to grow and develop. With so much to offer visitors and residents alike, the future holds out much hope.

One thing remains to be mentioned. The event which spawned this book had another lasting consequence. As part of the Ninth Centenary Celebrations, a temporary exhibition of local interest featuring items gathered from Tain and the surrounding district was staged. It proved so successful that it was decided to make it a permanent collection and so Tain and

District Museum was born. The collection continued to grow over the years and with it the importance of the museum which acquired Museum Registration in 1992. Since 1994, Tain and District Museum Trust has operated Tain Through Time, a four-star Visitor Centre consisting of the Museum, the Pilgrimage Building and the St Duthus Collegiate Church and its old churchyard. This reprint is the result of collaboration between Tain and District Museum, Tain Bookshop and Birlinn Ltd.

Changes in funding allocation have created difficulties for the Trust over the last two years. The original issue of *Tain Through the Centuries* was well received and the book was highly commended for its research and presentation in a notice in the *Scottish Historical Review* in 1968. It is our hope that this edition will be as successful. There must be a whole new generation of Tainites scattered across the globe who, as they get older, would welcome the chance to know more of their home town's history. Also there are many descendents of Tain folk who know little of the place their ancestors came from. This book will not only satisfy these needs but its purchase will help Tain and District Museum preserve Tain's rich and varied history.

Tain and District Museum
April 2005

(Photo: Beaverbrook Newspapers)

HER MAJESTY THE QUEEN . . .

. . . photographed outside the Town House during her visit to Tain on 25th June 1964, with Provost Robert Hay and General Sir Richard O'Connor, H.M. Lieutenant for Ross and Cromarty.

THE ROYAL BURGH OF TAIN
drawn on the spot by J. Clark (from an engraving by Robert Havell published in 1828)

Council Chambers,
TAIN, Ross-shire

This year we are celebrating the 900th Anniversary of the time when, according to tradition, Malcolm Canmore first conferred special trading privileges on the people of Tain. We are naturally very proud of our antiquity as a community and as a Burgh, and it is only fitting that we should welcome this opportunity to remind ourselves and others of it. Unfortunately the burning of St. Duthus' Chapel in 1427, with the destruction of our records, has left us with scanty sources of information. Thus it was decided that the 900th Anniversary would be an appropriate time to produce a new History of Tain, which we feel sure will be welcomed not only by people of Tain but by many in far-away places who know and love our Royal Burgh.

To undertake the work we were fortunate in obtaining two writers well versed in Highland history and genealogy — Mr R. W. Munro, F.S.A. SCOT., a journalist born in Ross-shire, and his wife, who is an honours graduate in history and a PH.D. of Edinburgh University. Their combined knowledge of published and unpublished sources, supplemented by a special study of the burgh and national records, has ensured a background of information and above all a detachment which should give the book a place of its own among the published histories of our Highland burghs. Moreover, their search for further details on the spot (including, I am told, an attempt to trace the boundaries of the old burgh lands in a midwinter snowstorm) has brought useful local colour into their account, for instance, of the perambulation of the marches.

The unfolding story reminds us more than once of the way in which Tain has built up connections all over the world. We read of a Tain plantation in what has become the new state of Guyana and of the St. Duthus School for girls in Canterbury near Melbourne, which was called after our own Saint. The fact that the two last names on our Roll of Freemen are Peter Fraser, late Prime Minister of New Zealand and the Hon. Frank Mackenzie Ross, former Lieutenant-Governor of

3

British Columbia, shows that new links are being forged in our own day.

I am certain that anyone interested in the history of the Highlands and the development of the royal and ancient burghs of Scotland, will welcome this book. In commending this book especially to all Tain folk and to all former pupils of Tain Royal Academy, wherever they may be, I would like to remind them that they carry with them some part of the old tradition of our Royal Burgh, and to assure them that they will always be made welcome when they return to it.

ROBERT HAY,
Provost

ACKNOWLEDGEMENTS

FOR information, loan of documents, and help of various kinds we wish to thank the Provost, Magistrates and Town Council of Tain; the Town Clerk, Mr H. W. Munro, and Burgh Surveyor, Mr W. R. McGregor; Mrs Carter, Mr W. H. Cormack, Mr George Hamilton, Mr and Mrs A. G. Melvin, Mrs W. J. Munro and Mrs Mackenzie, Mr A. G. R. Robertson, Miss Rosa R. Williamson Ross of Pitcalnie, and Mr A. H. V. Smyth, all of Tain; Mr William Hunter (factor at Balnagown), and Mr P. S. Leask (County Architect, Dingwall); the Rev. R. W. A. Begg, for a copy of his notice of Tain prepared for the Third Statistical Account; Dr William Ferguson, for perusal of his unpublished thesis on 'Electoral Law and Procedure in Eighteenth and early Nineteenth Century Scotland'; Mr R. J. Adam for his transcript of the 'Kalendar of Fearn'; and the Staff of the Scottish Record Office and the Signet Library, Edinburgh. We are particularly grateful to Mr W. H. Cormack, Mr Grant G. Simpson and Mr A. S. Munro for many helpful comments.

Footnotes have been kept to a minimum, but we propose to deposit fully annotated and referenced copies of the book with the Town Clerk of Tain and the Scottish Record Office in Edinburgh.

R.W.M.   J.M.

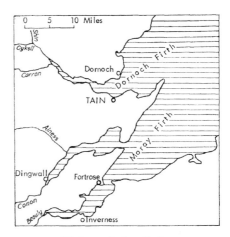

Tain and the firths

TAIN stands, as it has stood through the centuries, between
the heather and the sea, in the far north-east of Scotland,
where the ocean bites a great wedge-shaped chunk out of the
land.

Towards the open sea the edge of this triangle of water is
some seventy-five miles long, and each of the two coastwise
sides is about the same length. Into the western or landward
angle two promontories jut out, one oval in outline with a
hogbacked surface, and the other a jumble of hills narrowing
and lowering towards the sea, and ending in a sort of hammer-
head of which the claw is a long low tapering point of land.

Such, roughly, is the outline of what we call the Moray
Firth, with the Black Isle and the promontory of Ross at its
head. These two are bounded by three 'drowned' river valleys
— on the south, the irregular Inverness or Beauly Firth, which
runs fifteen miles inland from an entrance almost closed by two
long sandspits; in the middle, the spacious deep-water harbour

5

of the Cromarty Firth, its access from the sea less than a mile wide and guarded by two rocky headlands or Sutors; and on the north the winding Dornoch Firth, shallow and encumbered with sandbanks, which nearly join each other at its mouth.

Although it lies well within the Highland area, some geographers call the edges of this triangle the Moray Firth lowlands, for here the soil is fertile, the open sea is near, and there is little of the wetness of the hill country farther west. The climate is unique in Scotland, with mainly cool but sunny weather, and the rainfall only about 25 inches in the year. It is a pocket — or series of pockets — of low country tucked away beyond the Highland line, linked inescapably by land with the hills behind it, but also with its neighbours and the outer world by the sea.

Extensive raised beaches fringe the Cromarty and Dornoch Firths. On the brow of one of these natural terraces, or perhaps at first near the river mouth just below it — at any rate, somewhere 'between the heather and the sea' — the town of which this book tells the story was established.

It is a site of striking character and wide prospects. Behind rises a hill formed of old red sandstone, just over 900 feet high and encircled by the sea to the north and inland by two burns whose valleys almost join each other; beyond them is more heather and brown moorland, and to the west again the massive bulk of Ben Wyvis and its outliers separate the two rivers which flow into the Dornoch and Cromarty Firths, through valleys which open their separate ways to the western ocean. In front, below the terrace, a narrow strip of sandy links spreads out to the brink of the sea, or when the tide is low to a broad expanse of foreshore; through this a river meanders among the darker patches of the mussel 'scalps' until it is lost in the salt water, near the spot where the waves break on a sandy bar which almost joins the opposite coast; above, to the north, rises a further line of distant hills, with another lofty mountain on the skyline; while to the right, over a level plain of rough macharland, blown sand and shallow water, a low line of land runs out to a faraway point, with open sea beyond.

Some of our oldest surviving place-names are those describing the hills and rivers, glens and coasts of Scotland, as the natural features of land and sea are generally the first parts of a new country to be named.

Various attempts have been made to explain the name of Tain, of which the earliest written forms are Tene, Thayne, Thayn, Tayne and Tayn. The very simplicity of the word has made it all the more baffling, and opened the door to speculation. All that need be said is that modern philologists reject a derivation from the Norse *thing* or meeting-place, and believe it to have been originally a river-name. Some would derive it from the Gaelic, but the latest writer on the subject favours an even earlier origin, which would relate it to an early Celtic or Western Indo-European linguistic stratum existing in the British Isles with parallels on the Continent.

This at once raises the question — from which some of the speculation has naturally arisen — of what people first became familiar enough with this region to give names to its principal features. Here, although the picture is still uncertain, there are some generally accepted outlines which tell us something of the early pattern. When Ptolemy of Alexandria wrote his account of Britain in the first century of the Christian era, the ruling people in this region were Celts, who themselves had been incomers from the Continent. Their predecessors in earlier ages have left their mark on the northern landscape in hill forts such as the great Dùn in Strathrory and in chambered tombs of the kind which have been found under cairns of stone at the Red Burn near Edderton and the Dead Man's Cairn in Logie Easter, to name some of the older sites in the vicinity of Tain. These cairns lie usually on 'marginal' land between the rocky hills and the rich low-lying coastal plain, which would then support pretty dense forest probably of birch: they are noticeably absent from the parishes of Fearn and Tarbat.

From these early Celtic immigrants were descended the Picts, whose northern Kingdom had its centre near Inverness. They are remembered in the Tain area by the symbol-stones at Edderton and elsewhere and by several farm-names beginning with the characteristically Pictish prefix *Pit-* (meaning parcel of land). The outer fringes of the British Isles were then closely in touch with each other, and more than one Christian missionary from Ireland made his way to our Highland area. St. Columba visited the Pictish king Brude soon after the year 563, the early steps towards founding an ecclesiastical capital at Rosemarkie may have been taken not long after, and Maelrubha came to Applecross on the west coast in the seventh century. The faith which they established in Easter Ross is symbolised by a remarkable series of highly decorated cross slabs found in the area round Tain, at Shandwick, Nigg and Hilton.

One of the reasons why our knowledge of this period is scanty compared with other parts of Scotland is that the Romans did not penetrate so far north, although their 'eagles' may have been seen by the people living across the firth in Moray. But other invaders, from the Scandinavian lands, have left written accounts of their journeyings. Maelrubha is said to have fallen victim to the Viking raiders at Urquhart in Ross seventy years before Iona was sacked at the end of the eighth century. The Norse pirates were followed by settlers who voyaged 'west-over-sea' to Scotland when Harald Fairhair assumed the kingship of all Norway and caused discontent and opposition among the lesser kinglets. Some reached our east coast direct from Norway, and others by way of the northern isles or other places; objects found in Viking graves suggest colonisation from Orkney during the tenth century, and one hoard of silver dug up at Tarbat included Saxon and Frankish coins.

Among the most influential Norse chiefs was Sigurd, Earl of Orkney, who invaded the mainland and conquered as far as the Oykell river about 890. By this time the Picts had been united with the Scots under Kenneth MacAlpin, and the capital had been moved to Dunkeld; but in Easter Ross the Norse continued to occupy the low-lying lands — as far south as Beauly, if place-name evidence is to be trusted — for something like two centuries, while the Picts for the most part remained in the hills. About 980 another Earl Sigurd, known as 'the Stout', who had an Irish mother and half-Irish father, tried to claim Caithness as well as Orkney, and after having failed he threw in his lot with Malcolm II and helped him to subdue Moray. He even married the king's daughter, and their son Thorfinn (born about 1008) was a contemporary of the first-named — although still shadowy — native of Tain, a saint whose memory still stands high.

There must, it seems certain, have been some Christian settlement at Tain when 'the kind confessor blessed St. Duthac' was born there; in fact, it may already have become a place of importance in the North. Nothing recorded about St. Duthac during his lifetime has come down to us, and we must grope among later sources for any knowledge of him, but the variety of information surely indicates how wide was the range of his influence.

It is the account-book of a royal pilgrim that tells us of Duthac's birth on the little mound below the town where the chapel named after him still stands (the ambiguous wording of the entry even led to the belief that James IV himself was born there). His parentage is unknown, but we are assured that he sprang from no ignoble family, and was early imbued by wise instructors in the Christian faith. In the flowering of his youth (according to a Prior of St. Andrews, writing for the papal ear) Duthac shone like the morning star in the midst of a cloud. And the worthy Bishop Elphinstone, after moving from the See of Ross to Aberdeen, gave his sanction to the story of an early miracle: telling how the boy was sent for some fire to a smithy, and when the heartless smith snatched up a quantity of coals with the tongs and thrust them into his lap, he carried them safely to his master without damage to himself or his clothes.

Then (according to the same authority) by divine direction Duthac crossed to Ireland, where he betook himself to the study of the precepts and laws of both Old and New Testaments. On his return he taught publicly with all gentleness, proving himself an outstanding confessor of God by his preaching, and a genuine Christian by his life and conversation. As his fame and reputation grew (says the poetic prior) crowds gathered from all sides to hear him, men were led to holiness and the truth of the Christian faith, devotion was increased, the Lord was praised for His saving grace, and thanks given to the Author of Salvation. He was (in a seventeenth century writer's phrase) 'a very godlie man'.

We live in a more sceptical age than Duthac's or even Elphinstone's, and it is harder for us to recapture the atmosphere of miracle-working, 'even against the course of nature', in which Duthac 'glittered as in the shining rays of the sun'. Despising alike the applause of princes and of people, the holy man was praised for his simplicity and humility. He shunned company, banqueting and all worldly comfort, but a story tells the outcome of one feast to which he apparently went. A fellow-guest, finding himself unable to eat his portion of pork owing to a sick headache, sent it to his own house by one of Duthac's disciples, with a gold ring presumably as a talisman. On the way he stopped at a cemetery to pray for the souls of those buried there, and no sooner had he laid down the meat and the ring than a hungry kite swooped down and flew away with them to a dense wood on the other side of a river. In fear of the anger of both the owner and his master, the disciple went back and told what had happened. Duthac retired, and after a few minutes' prayer the kite returned and laid what he had taken at his feet; while accepting the ring the saint restored the meat to the bird, which joyfully flew away.

Food is again the subject of two other miraculous tales which Bishop Elphinstone thought suitable for his flock. A canon of the church of Dornoch, in celebrating the feast of St. Finbar (of Cork), ordered a fat ox to be killed for the poor; when he took a portion to Duthac the night was dark and stormy, but the spit on which he carried the meat gave forth a light both coming and going. On another occasion, through the saint's intervention, the remains of a cake made with honey and butter worked miracles of healing.

Just what authority Duthac held during his lifetime is uncertain, and the accounts differ. Later churchmen were proud to call him 'bishop', sometimes of Ross and even of St. Andrews, but he does not seem to have been one at least in the strictly ecclesiastical sense. Recording his death in the year 1065 at Armagh — the great religious centre established by

St. Patrick — the Irish chroniclers called him *Dubhtach Albannach*, chief soul-friend or confessor (*prim Anmchara, praecipuus confessarius*) of Erin and Alba. His last words, according to a legend which even a Presbyterian writer thought might here have caught up a true tradition, were: '*Quae est expectatio mea? nonne Dominus?*' ('What wait I for now but for Thee, O Lord?')

However much of these stories may be true, such is the picture of St. Duthac which was venerated by the churchmen of later times, no doubt in Tain as well as Aberdeen and elsewhere. Now we must glance (more cursorily) at what was going on in the North of Scotland in his day. Young Thorfinn, his contemporary, grew up under the mighty shadow of his father Earl Sigurd, who was killed at the battle of Clontarf in Ireland (1014); he obtained possession, says the *Orkneyinga Saga*, of nine Scottish earldoms (certainly including Ross) and all the Hebrides, as well as a large territory in Ireland, which made him potentially the most powerful subject of the King of Scots in the North.

Malcolm II was Thorfinn's grandfather, and after victory over the English at Carham (1016 or 1018) had secured his southern boundary the king was free to turn his attention elsewhere. He showed some encouragement to Thorfinn, but his grandson Duncan, during his few years as king, claimed tribute from the earl, whose refusal to pay led to war in Ross by land and sea. Trouble continued during the reign of Macbeth — who like Duncan was Thorfinn's cousin — and there was also internal trouble in Orkney and Shetland, which Thorfinn held of the Norwegian king. He married Ingibjorg, daughter of Finn Arnason and first cousin of the Queen of Norway, and in his later years laid aside his warlike ways and even visited the pope (St. Leo IX) at Rome in 1050. On Thorfinn's death, a year or so before St. Duthac, the lands he held as a Norseman were divided between his sons, and according to the saga his nine Scottish earldoms 'fell away and went under those men who were territorially born to rule over them'.

Tain has a connection with the great Earl Thorfinn because Malcolm Canmore, the son of Duncan and King of Scots after the death of Macbeth in 1057, married Ingibjorg, either his widow or his daughter. Not only was Ross numbered among his Scottish earldoms, but also it is known that Malcolm II — Thorfinn's grandfather and Canmore's great-grandfather — had looked with favour on young Thorfinn. It is more than likely that Malcolm would visit the northern lands which Thorfinn held of the Scottish crown, as we are soon to hear of other kings who unquestionably found their way to Easter Ross.

Malcolm III, surnamed '*Ceann mor*' or 'big head', reigned from 1058 to 1093. His second wife, the saintly Saxon princess Margaret, is the one of whom history has most to say, but his earlier marriage to Ingibjorg is more important in relation to the founding of Tain. As Thorfinn died in 1064 or 1065, and the marriage with Margaret took place about 1068 or 1070, Malcolm's attention might well have been directed sometime between 1064 and 1068 towards Ross and the other wide possessions held by the earl. In fact, one modern historian thinks it likely that this marriage was contracted in an attempt to secure the friendship of the Norsemen in the northern parts of the mainland, possibly even to recover the 'nine earldoms' which the Scottish crown is said to have lost to Thorfinn.

According to tradition, King Malcolm gave to all dwellers within the 'liberty' (*immunitas*) of Tain, which he first founded, the privilege of buying and selling goods within the 'four corner crosses' without contribution to the king beyond the usual customs, and of sailing with their merchandise where-ever they wished; and he is also said to have recognised that they were under the special protection of the apostolic see.

These points appear in a 16th century copy of an inquest held at Tain in 1439 (see chapter 4), and no trace has survived in the public records either of the original grant by Malcolm or of confirmations said to have been given by Robert Bruce and his successors. From the document it appears that 23 local men were ordered to define the privileges enjoyed by their town — possibly following the destruction of older records, although it is unlikely that Malcolm would have granted any formal charter, and there was probably no written evidence dating from his reign. It has been claimed that the document proves that Malcolm made Tain a royal burgh, but this is not so. It is true that similar trading privileges were an important part of burgh status, but equally essential was the right to hold a burgh court administering its own special law, which Tain apparently did not claim.

The reign of Malcolm ended nearly 30 years before the earliest known date of any Scottish royal burgh (though many do not know the exact date of their foundation), and the idea of establishing burghs is usually associated with the Norman influence of Malcolm's youngest son King David. But by 1439 burgh status was generally recognised and understood, and it would have been a simple matter to claim it for Tain without discussing detailed trading rights and the protection of the apostolic see. The fact that burgh status was not mentioned in 1439 is one of the strongest arguments for believing that it was not even then enjoyed by Tain, although the privileges claimed to have been granted by Malcolm and confirmed by later kings might well be appropriate to a community based on the sanctuary or *immunitas* of Tain.

2

St. Duthac's chapel

ALTHOUGH the 'four corner crosses' of the girth or sanctuary of St. Duthac have disappeared, like those which marked out other sanctuaries in Scotland, we know just where three of them stood and we can make a fair guess at the site of the fourth. The exact area which they enclosed cannot now be measured with absolute certainty, but it must have been within a trapezium something over twelve square miles in extent that the law of the medieval church would protect a fugitive against arrest or violence.

The first cross stood about a mile north-east from Tain, on what was known as Paul McTyre's Hill, which can no longer be distinguished either because the sea has encroached on the land at this point or else because the sand which formed it has been dispersed. St. Katherine's Cross stood about half-way along the north shore of Loch Eye, on a small conical mound near a modern house which uses the old name. Still moving in a sunwise direction, the next stood somewhere near the foot of

Scotsburn Glen, below Culpleasant and north of the hill of Bearns a' Chlaidheimh ('Barnsclay'). The fourth cross stood on the north side of Edderton Hill, at the great cairn beside the Red Burn (Allt Dearg) and about half a mile above the main road.[1] All four sites are peaceful and accessible enough today, but one writer was prompted to remark that the confluence of scoundrels attracted by this holy girth — nearly as large as the modern parish — must have invested life in medieval Tain with many exciting features.

All that we know of events in Easter Ross during the centuries which followed the death of Duthac bears out the impression that they were troubled times. The Malcolm-Ingibjorg marriage is said to have secured peace for thirty years, but when the king was killed on his last invasion of England in 1093 the old concept of the succession of an adult male collateral came into conflict with the new idea of inheritance by primogeniture, and another dynastic squabble broke out. Those who opposed the advance of English influence chose Malcolm's brother to be King, while his eldest son by Ingibjorg marched north with Anglo-Norman aid and held the throne for a brief period as Duncan II; he was killed and Donald Bane ruled in his stead, followed by Edgar, Malcolm's son by Queen Margaret. In these confused waters King Magnus of Norway fished happily, but his success in the west was not matched in the north, where the Kings of Scots gradually gained power and acceptance in their own kingdom through the influence of local magnates.

Some of these events came very close to Tain, if not actually into its sanctuary, in the twelfth century. Alexander I, his brother David, and the latter's son William the Lion all had to contend with opposition from descendants of Duncan II. The spirit of rebellion was strongest in the North, but even the monks of Melrose heard of and recorded the march of royal

1 The sites of the fourth girth crosses are established by the following references (taken along with the 1750 maps mentioned in chapter 8):—(1) W. Macgill, *Old Ross-shire*, nos. 1229, 1239. (2) Macgill, no. 1219; Ordnance Survey map (6 ins. to mile) and 1871 notes. (3) *Register of the Great Seal*, 28 July, 1617; W. J. Watson, *Place-Names of Ross and Cromarty*, pp. 32, 60, 62; Macgill, no. 908. (4) Macgill, nos. 1210, 1219, 1239. The name of the first is said to be taken from Paul McTyre, 'a man of great power and possessions' in the 14th century, who built Dun Creich.

armies into Ross to quell disorders. The great castles of Dunskaith — perched on a crag above the King's Ferry at Nigg, the revenues from which helped to secure its upkeep — and Edirdowyr (Redcastle in the Black Isle) were built and strengthened. Further trouble followed the death of William and the accession of Alexander II in 1214, but the insurgent leaders were seized by Ferquhard, a powerful Highland chief who was apparently son to the lay parson of Applecross. 'He cut off their heads and presented them as gifts to the new king', wrote the Melrose chronicler gruesomely, and was rewarded with a knighthood and later created Earl of Ross.

It was at Tain that Ferquhard — a national figure and the first of five earls who succeeded each other from father to son — died in 1252, but he was buried in the abbey of Fearn which he had founded. Tain was a place of some importance ecclesiastically — the body of St. Duthac himself is said to have been 'translated' there in 1253 — but there is no word of a residence fit for an earl in it; Ferquhard and his successors lived at the castles of Delny or Dingwall, and it was at the latter that their charters were dated when the earldom, by descent through an heiress, was held by the Macdonald Lords of the Isles.

Tain and its sanctuary came into unwelcome prominence in the difficult times of the War of Independence. The Bishops of Ross and Moray were on Bruce's side, but the Earl of Ross (who was married to a Comyn) at first opposed him in the struggle for the crown. King Edward of England came north with an army — he reached Kinloss just across the Moray Firth in 1303, and Cromarty Castle is believed to have held out against a long siege by his forces. By the summer of 1306, although by now a crowned king, Bruce's fortunes were at a low ebb, and he sent the Queen and princess Marjorie for safety to the castle of Kildrummy. It too was threatened by the English, and the royal ladies were sent hurriedly northward, probably in charge of the Earl of Atholl. They may have planned to seek refuge in Orkney, but unfortunately they had to pass through the territory of the Earl of Ross, and the first appearance in history of St. Duthac's sanctuary is a sorry tale. Barbour's *Bruce* tells how they rode.

16

'With knychtis and with squyeris bath,
Throw Ross, rycht to the gyrth of Tayne.
Bot that travaill thai maid in vayne;
For thai off Ross, that wald nocht ber
For thaim na blayme, na yheit (yet) danger,
Owt off the gyrth thame all has tayne;
And syne has send thaim evirilkane
Rycht intill Ingland, to the King,
That girt draw all men, and hing;
And put the ladyis in presoune,
Sum intill castell, sum in dongeoun.'

This is not the only known instance of the sanctuary being violated, but in the others the cause seems to have been greed and the temptation offered by the rich possessions of the church. Sometime in the middle or later part of the fourteenth century — the date is uncertain — a band of lawless Maclennans are said to have pillaged both Tain and the Chanonry of Ross.

An even worse disaster befell the shrine of St. Duthac soon after James I returned from his English exile full of determination to curb the trouble-makers. The king was to meet the Highland chiefs at Inverness in 1428, and it seems to have been just before he came that Alexander Mowat, Laird of Freswick, was returning to Caithness from the south. He had a feud with the owner of Creich and other lands on the north side of the Dornoch Firth, Thomas Mackay the son of Neil; at Tain, says one of the two Highland chroniclers who relate the story, Mowat 'would pay his vow to St. Duthus, and being at his devotion Thomas Mckneil surprises them, and killed him in the very chappell, which he also burnt, to which Alex. Mowat retired as to a very sanctuary'. When the king heard of this, Thomas was at once proclaimed a rebel, and, being betrayed by his own brothers, he was executed at the castle hill of Inverness. As a warning to others, the murderer's limbs were dispersed, and 'his right hand set up at Tain, a horrid spectacle'; in 1430 his brother Neil received as a reward the lands of Creich which Thomas forfeited.

17

This burning of St. Duthac's chapel was of concern to others besides the unlucky victim and the clergy immediately affected. The white canons of Fearn, whose abbey had been founded near Edderton about two centuries earlier by Earl Ferquhard, had moved before the thirteenth century was out to a site within five miles of the chapel of St. Duthac. This flitting, it has been pointed out, put the sanctuary of Tain between the abbey and the wild Highlanders of Kincardine parish — a wise precaution for an order which combined services in parish churches and manual labour with their own religious observances. Not content with that, the abbot seems to have entrusted his most precious records to the chapel for safe keeping: for a new charter granted in 1467 records that the abbey's foundation charter, the papal bull of confirmation, and other deeds, together with numerous relics, were reduced to ashes with St. Duthac's chapel. It is also sad to think that some of the early documents relating to Tain may have perished at the same time, for the town's oldest charter now extant (1587/8) says that their 'old infeftments and charters were cruelly burnt in a fire caused by certain savage and rebellious Ersch [Gaelic] subjects'.

But the picture cannot have been one of unrelieved gloom, of a sanctuary that was never a safe refuge. Just as the newspapers of our own day give prominence to the exceptional rather than the normal, so we may suppose that many fugitives found safety when they sought it for every one who suffered by its violation.

One who remained safely in Tain for several years, although accused of treason against James III along with the king's brother Albany, was William Lord Crichton. Himself a low-lander, Crichton had family connections in the North: his father (son of James II's chancellor) was at one time Earl of Moray in right of his wife, who was also heiress of Dunbeath and other lands in Caithness. As a part of a process of for-feiture against him, a macer or messenger summoned him by proclamation at the market crosses of Banff, Elgin, Forres, Nairn and Inverness without getting any certain knowledge of his whereabouts. Someone must have talked, however, for on the last day of 1483 the messenger passed 'to the town of Thane in Ross, where the Lord Creichtoun lived in the vicar's house', and summoned his lordship to appear in parliament at Edinburgh to answer for his treason. Witnesses included a bailie of Tain (William Johnsoun) and of Cromarty, a burgess of Inverness, and Lord Crichton's 'brother and familiar follower' Alexander Sutherland. Failing to appear, he was forfeited and outlawed in his absence; and although parlia‚ ment knew where he was lodged no further action is recorded‚ and it is not known how, when or where he died.

By this time the earldom of Ross had fallen to the crown through the repeated rebellion of its holders, who as Lords of the Isles acted the part of independent sovereigns. Donald of Harlaw had claimed the earldom to which his wife was heiress, and had fought for it against the king's own forces. His son Alexander of the Isles had also rebelled, begged for clemency at Holyroodhouse, and been reinstated after a spell in Tan‚ tallon castle. In January 1436, as Earl of Ross and Lord of the Isles, he granted the lands of Scardy, Plaids and others, and the office of 'baillie of the immunity of Tain' to Alexander Mac‚ Culloch by a charter dated at the castle of Dingwall. The same office — it was to last for more than 300 years — was held in 1458 by John McCulloch, to whom Earl John addressed a letter as 'bailie of the girth of Sanct Duthowis'.

At this time the earl was at peace with King James, but it was not long before he was back at the old intrigues. These reached a peak with the so-called treaty of Ardtornish (or Westminster-Ardtornish) of 1462, by which he promised his own and his followers' allegiance to Edward IV of England and their support in his wars against the Scots. It was some time before this came to light, but Ross was probably involved in its earl's rebellion along with other parts of the North. He was himself at Tain on 12th April 1463, when he put his seal to a charter (the only one known by an Earl of Ross which has Tain as its place of origin) to Donald Corbatt of the lands of Easter Arde. The list of witnesses — Finlay Abbot of Fearn, William Thane of Cawdor, John Munro of Foulis, and even a Maclean from Mull and MacQuarrie of Ulva — suggests that he still had his army, or at any rate his council, around him.

The inevitable eventually happened. Forfeited in 1475, he was later pardoned but forced to surrender the earldom of Ross, which was annexed to the crown and appointed to remain with the king's second son. At Edinburgh in July 1476 John Lord of the Isles put his seal — now showing only the galley with double tressure, no longer quartered with the three lions rampant of Ross — to a terse but comprehensive renunciation of the earldom and the offices of sheriff of Inverness and Nairn, binding himself and his heirs never to offer any impediment or obstacle to the king, his chamberlains, officers, servants and vassals, etc. His father's humiliation in the sanctuary of Holyrood may have been more abject, but it could not have been more complete. As the galley of the Isles sailed back into the Hebridean mists, severing a 200-year-old link with the sanctuary of St. Duthac and the town which was growing up beside it, there were signs that a new epoch was already beginning for the church and community of Tain.

3

Collegiate church

Ross was one of the three northern dioceses of Scotland in the Middle Ages, and, like its neighbours to the north and south — Caithness and Moray — it took its name from the province and not from the town in which its cathedral church was built. From the Hill of Tain, as it happens, you can still see Dornoch Cathedral across the firth, once the heart of the See of Caithness and now largely rebuilt; on a clear day it might almost have been possible to glimpse the twin towers of the sister church at Elgin, glory of the bishopric of Moray; but the rounded ridge of the Black Isle hides from view the Cathedral Church of Ross, of which enough remains in the burgh of Fortrose to show that it must have been 'an architectural gem of the very first description'.

In the absence of diocesan and cathedral records, we can form a general idea of the diocese of Ross. Tain was one of its 35 parishes, all on the mainland, stretching from Tarbat in the east to Applecross in the west. Under the bishop were four principal dignitaries — the dean, preceptor, chancellor and treasurer — and several lesser ones, and with them a body of about twenty canons formed the chapter of Ross. Each had for his maintenance an allowance derived from the revenues of some parish church or churches in the diocese (where he was obliged to support a resident vicar), those of Tain and Edderton being enjoyed by the sub-dean. In addition, there were sanctuaries protected by the influence of the Church at Applecross and Tain, and two of the religious orders had establishments in the North — a priory of the Valliscaulians at Beauly, and an abbey of the Premonstratensians or White Canons at Fearn.

The reputation of St. Duthac and his sanctuary ensured that Tain would not sink to the level of a forgotten parish, solely dependent on the services of a poorly rewarded vicar. The 'translation' of Duthac's body from Armagh to Tain is recorded in 1253, showing that Tain was regarded as worthy of honour, and that its sanctity was to be increased. As was only fitting, it long treasured various personal relics of the saint — 'ane heid of silver callit sanct Duthois hede', his breast-bone, his shirt (supposed to protect its wearer from death or injury), his cup and his bell.

But an important step in advancing the importance of Tain as an ecclesiastical centre was taken by Robert the Bruce himself. In allowing an amnesty to William Earl of Ross, who had handed John of Atholl over to execution (probably when the Queen was taken), the king expressly stipulated that Ross should 'maintain at his own expense six chaplains to say masses for Earl John at St. Duthac's church'. The English too must have had an inkling of Tain's reputation, for when the next Earl of Ross was killed at Halidon Hill, in spite of wearing the miraculous shirt, they thoughtfully returned it. A member of the great house of Douglas, too, is said to have had the pious intention of leaving one of his robes to be added to the sanctuary's vestments, although there is some doubt whether this was ever carried out.

The records of the day show that Duthac was accorded the title of 'saint' long before it was formally conferred by the apostolic see. It was Archibald Earl of Douglas who, both by special envoy and by letters, represented to Pope Martin V his suitability for canonisation. This was described as the wish of the entire Scottish people in the humble petition drawn up by James Haldenstone, Prior of St. Andrews, probably soon after visiting Rome in 1418.[1] While not wishing to weary His Holiness by recounting the candidate's many miracles, enough was said to show the nationwide fame which he had achieved.

Precedent required — as the eloquent prior well knew — that many careful and exact inquiries must be made before a new name was added to the roll of saints; that Duthac's survived the inquisition may be presumed from the fact that it has long been allotted a place in the Roman calendar under the 8th of March. Bishop Elphinstone, whose brief tenure of the See of Ross before he went to Aberdeen is worth remembering, selected nine passages on the life of St. Duthac from Irish and Scottish writings and legends to be recited in his diocese on that day.

Tain took its place among other religious centres in the North when, in 1456, Alexander Sutherland of Dunbeath directed that it should be one of the six places where masses should be said for his soul (the total of 30 successive masses was made up by having 8 in Chanonry, 4 each in Fearn, Tain, Dornoch and Kinloss, and 6 in Orkney). This Caithness laird, who was married to a sister of Alexander Earl of Ross and Lord of the Isles, evidently had lodgings ('ynnys') of a kind in Tain, where he is on record as leaving three 'kists' full of gear.

A year later came the first sign of devotion by a Stewart monarch to Tain and its saint. At Inverness on 10th October, 1457, James II endowed a chaplaincy in the parish church in honour of the Virgin Mary, the blessed Duthac confessor, and for the souls of his father, his mother and his own queen. The charter, witnessed by John Earl of Ross and Lord of the Isles, speaks of 'ecclesia collegiata S. Duthaci de Tayne', and directs that the chaplain is to celebrate mass daily at the high altar, and at the beginning of each to exhort the people to say a *pater noster* with a *Salutacione Angelica* and to be present in the choir at matins, high mass, and vespers in his habit like the other chaplains of the church. For his maintenance the lands of

1 Copiale Prioratus Sanctiandree, ed. J. H. Baxter, pp. 4-6, 385.

Dunskaith were allocated, and also two merks from the profits of the king's ferry from Cromarty to Nigg.

As the number of its clergy grew, St. Duthac's church at Tain gradually came to have a communal existence. This is made plain by the use, rather prematurely, of the term 'collegiate', which is also used in referring to a grant by the Earl of Ross before 1468 of a mill and lands — evidently those of Morangie — to support a sacrist. In 1482, James III followed his father's example by endowing a chaplainry at St. Duthac's to say masses for the souls of his father, mother and wife, and gave the lands of Newmore to Thomas Monelaw and his successors as chaplains.

Masses were said for the souls of lesser folk as well as for royal personages. In June 1487 Thomas Ross, sub-dean of the cathedral church, granted to 'the chaplains and deacons' of the church of St. Duthac the lands of Priestown commonly called 'Balnasagyrde', lying within the lands of Tain and near the king's way; sixteen plough oxen and two horses belonging to these lands; and a further 'croft' of land. The first grant was for the welfare of his own soul and those of William Ross of Easter Kindeace, his own mother, and all the faithful departed; the second to pay for one mass for the queen every seventh day on all the Mondays at the altar of St. Marie in the parish church of Tain and after vespers for the safety of the queen; and the third was for the celebration of 'our obit' (or death anniversary) likewise annually at the altar of St. Marie. For performing these duties the clerks were to be paid two shillings in the year, twelve pennies at Pentecost and twelve at St. Martin.

Finally, the chapel of Saint Duthac of Tayne, bishop, confessor, and priest, was erected in 1487 into a collegiate church for a provost, five canons, two deacons or sub-deacons, a sacrist with an assistant clerk, and three singing boys. This was done with the assent of his chapter by Thomas Hay, Bishop of Ross, at the instance of James III, for the weal of his soul and of the souls of his predecessors and successors kings of Scotland, and of all who had contributed anything towards the foundation, by a charter dated 12th September, which passed the Great Seal on 3rd December.

Many of these collegiate churches were founded in Scotland during the fifteenth century, but they had no connection with education. They were, in fact, incorporated bodies of clergy whose primary function was to sing masses for the souls of the founder (in this case the king himself), his family, friends and heirs in perpetuity. The 'college' was thus basically a glorified chantry, but the service attained a beauty and dignity which was impossible with only one priest. As in cathedrals, the usual daily services were provided, but on a smaller scale.

Although subject to some supervision by his bishop, the provost of a collegiate church was a man with wide powers and responsibilities. In Tain, he was invested with full ecclesiastical authority over all his clergy, and also full jurisdiction over them, their familiars and servitors dwelling in the town of Tain. He could suspend or excommunicate any of them, and he also had the power of excommunication and absolution over the inhabitants of the three 'touns' — Tarlogie, Morangie and Cambuscurrie — within the girth of Tain whose teinds or tithes were granted (by consent of Thomas Ross, the rector of Tain) for maintaining the fabric of the church and repairing its ornaments and books, and the 'toun' of Newmore, recently added to the foundation by the king.

For his own maintenance the provost was given the vicarage of Tain, which he himself continued to hold, and the escheats (fines) of the courts of the town of Tain were also allotted to him.

The five canons or prebendaries, declared the charter, were to be regularly qualified priests, trained in morals, literature and especially singing. They were bound to be present with the other officials at matins, vespers and other canonical hours and masses, in good surplices made at their own expense, and to sing at the mass *De Corpore* etc. every Thursday. One of the five was to be chosen by the provost to preside in his absence, and to celebrate a private mass daily for the welfare (*status*) of the king, his ancestors and his successors.

Of the four other canons, one was to rule the choir in singing and to instruct the three choir boys; the two deacons or sub-deacons were to be regularly instructed and sufficiently qualified in singing and in literature; and the sacrist, also trained in singing and literature, was to have under him an assistant with a surplice and becoming dress, who should ring the bell and supply fire and water in the church. The charter laid down exactly how all these were to be maintained, and who was to appoint them. The five canons, for instance, drew their revenues from Newmore, Dunskaith, Tarlogie, Morangie and Cambuscurrie; the two deacons were to have for their maintenance six merks Scots each from the lands of Invereathie and Tain, and the choir boys were to be paid three merks or forty shillings Scots by John Munro of Foulis, John Merschell of Davochcarty, and the heirs of Andrew Alanesoun and their successors.

All these officials were bound continually to reside in the college, and not to be absent above eight days, or even so long without the licence of the provost or his deputy. Should they be longer absent, even in the courts of the king, the bishop or the earl, they would forfeit their offices — not even the pope himself could release them from continual residence. So much weight was attached to this that all had to swear obedience to these statutes, and especially to that relating to residence and the invalidity of any dispensation.

The first Provost of the Collegiate Church was Thomas Monelaw (or Monylawe), who had been chaplain of Newmore in 1482. Two years later, as perpetual vicar of the parish church of Tain and a notary public, he witnessed a charter by John Ross of Balnagown and other 'common citizens and clerks' of Tain. In 1486, while holding the same office, he granted property in the town to his cousin Donald Monelaw, with a William and John Monelaw among the witnesses. Thomas appears on record as provost a few months before the bishop's charter setting up the collegiate church (when he witnessed the grant by Thomas Ross already referred to), and again in October, 1487, but he was provost for not much longer than three years. His early disappearance from the records gave rise to the erroneous idea that he was dismissed but he actually died in office in January, 1491; and in recording his death the *Kalendar of Fearn* (a manuscript found at Dunrobin, and not yet printed in full) shows that he left the collegiate church richer by a silver head of St. Duthac. Monelaw's successor William Spynie held the office for more than twenty years, and his long provostship is memorable for Pope Innocent VIII's confirmation of the foundation carter of the collegiate church, and for the almost annual pilgrimages to the shrine of St. Duthac by King James IV.

Pope Innocent's bull of 1492 is one of the most treasured possessions of the Royal Burgh of Tain today. It measures only 14 inches by 9, and attached to it (by a silken cord in which red and yellow strands mingle, to show that it contains matter of justice as well as grace) is the original lead seal in perfect condition. The Pope himself could have had little if any part in the transaction, for he died only eight days later after a long and painful illness; but the parchment which carries his name in decorative capitals, 'INNOCENTUS', bears the signature of (and was perhaps prepared by) a man of even greater eminence — Alessandro Farnese, then cardinal-secretary, who later wore the triple crown as Paul III, and was the pope who excommunicated Henry VIII of England. The bull, dated at St. Peter's in Rome on 17th July, 1492, is addressed to William Spynie, provost of the church of the blessed Duthac of Tain, in Ross, on whose behalf the petition had been brought.

Gone now were the days when Tain boasted nothing but a hermit priest living the simple life in the chapel on the knoll whose ruins we know today. The hermit remained, as we learn from Tain's most famous pilgrim, but what had been the simple parish church on the terrace above had blossomed into a grander structure. The nave, with a choir very long in proportion, would still be used for parochial purposes, and the chancel would be enlarged to fit in with the church's collegiate status. The sacred relics, much venerated for themselves and also a valuable source of revenue, were kept in the 'revestre' when not in use, had an important place in the liturgy, and were carried in procession in costly reliquaries. There was also a chapter house where the clergy could convene to transact business, and a schoolhouse, but of both all trace has now disappeared. Some of the great walls to be seen nearby — said to be connected with the church by underground passages, and later to raise speculations about a dubious 'castle' — may have been part of the living quarters for the college clergy and their dependents, who must have formed a considerable community.

James IV came first to Tain as a young man of 21, on the threshold of a life which was to be devoted to solemn expiation (he blamed himself for having been accessory to his father's death five years earlier), culture and gaiety, and the improvement of his people's condition, in not unequal parts. Tantalisingly brief, but sometimes revealing, the records mention some 18 different visits from the first in October 1493 to the last in August 1513 — the month before he fell at Flodden. Four or five years in the sequence are blank, but it is by no means certain that what had become such a regular event did not take place in them as well.

It was for only a day or two at a time that the king 'lichtit' (alighted) at Tain, but sometimes (as in 1497) there were two visits in the same year, or even three; most of them were in the summer months, but he also made the journey at Easter and in March, October and November. This constant loyalty to St. Duthac's shrine is remarkable, for James also made an annual pilgrimage to Whithorn (at the other end of his kingdom), and frequently visited remote shrines such as that on the Isle of May, as well as looking after the interests of a country which needed a firm and vigilant monarch to rule over it.

There was, perhaps, some pleasure in moving about his kingdom with only a small escort, and beating for a day or two those who pursued him with the business of state. (There is record of only one charter which he granted while at Tain — a confirmation to Alexander Guthrie of some lands in Angus in 1511.) The king would usually come North by Aberdeen and Elgin — once he made a call at Kingussie — with some time for hunting or other entertainment on the way; then round the head of the firths by Inverness, Beauly and Dingwall, or across the ferries of Ardersier and Cromarty with pious halts at the Chanonry of Ross and Rosemarkie. Extra boats would be needed for his servants and gear, which on at least two occasions included a portable organ for use at Tain. Within a month of his marriage to Margaret Tudor, offerings were made at Tain for the king and queen, and she rode with him by way of Elgin on his Easter pilgrimage in 1510; but on other occasions he travelled light, rapidly and alone, as in that astonishing journey recorded by a later Bishop of Ross — those who experienced it may have told him of the royal hustle — when James rode in one day from Stirling through Perth and Aberdeen to Elgin (130 miles), slept on a table in his riding clothes, and after rising at daylight and covering another forty miles in the saddle, reached Tain in time to hear mass at St. Duthac's. On his last visit, according to local tradition, James passed barefoot along the stony track south of the town still known as the King's Causeway.

Just how much money was disbursed during these visits is known from accounts of the royal expenditure. In 1495 they record the first payment of £5 to be paid every half year to a chaplain to say masses for the soul of James III — for the priest (as later entries succinctly put it) 'that singis for the King in Tayne'. In Tain itself the main items were for offerings: there seem to have been five principal 'stances', and in 1506 the king handed out 14 shillings each (this was apparently the regular donation at a religious place) to the 'relics' on arrival, in the 'chappell be est Tayn', to the relics at the revestry, in the 'stok' of the town, and on the 'bred'. Then there was 5s. to the hermit at St. Duthac's chapel and to the pardoner with St. Duthac's cup, 4s. to the man that bore St. Duthac's 'cabok' (alb, shirt), 3s. to the man who carried St. Duthac's bell, and 2s. to the poor folk at the gate. In most years there was also even heavier expense in providing further 'relics' (or more probably reliquaries in which to keep them), when the value of the silver, the craftsman's fee, and the cost of gilding might total as much as £28 4s. For 'a cas of silver to the croce the King offerit to Sanct Duthow', weighing 9¼ oz., the goldsmith received £6 0s. 3d.; but another item shows that the cost of the precious metal at least might be saved by economical housekeeping, as one relic was made from 'ane of the auld silver platis brokin' containing 23½ oz.

From entries for 1498 and 1505, it appears that the king

lodged with the vicar of Tain (this was the provost of the collegiate church, William Spynie), and presumably the parish revenues would have to pay for maintaining the royal guest and his household. There are, however, payments for 'extras', which show that all was not solemnity and ceremonial: such as 28s. 'for the King's belcheir (entertainment) in Tayn', and 14s. to the laird of Balnagown's harper.

James V was less the pious pilgrim than his father, and as he was only an infant at the time of Flodden he was at first the pawn of his nobles. Among his early tutors was Sir David Lindsay, poet and herald, who may have told him of his father's devotion to images, such as

> 'Sanct ringane, of ane rottin stoke,
> Sanct Duthow, borit out of ane bloke,
> Sanct Andrew, with his croce in hand . . . .'

So great a concourse of pilgrims flocked to the shrines of the Scottish saints that even in England verse-makers wrote after Flodden of 'Saint Andrew with his shored croce' and Saint Ninian of 'Quhytehorn'. They even took such liberties with the name of one saint that those who venerated it would hardly recognise Duthac as

> 'Doffin, their demigod of Ross'.

These were increasingly hard days for the old religion, and there is a link between Easter Ross and the new ideas of Luther and Erasmus in the person of Patrick Hamilton, the first Scottish martyr of the Reformation. At the age of fourteen he received the revenues of the abbey of Fearn to enable him to study on the Continent, where he absorbed the new teachings so eagerly that he must propound them to his countrymen at home. Brought to loggerheads with the archbishop, he was summoned to St. Andrews in 1528 to answer for his faith; and by a strange coincidence, it is said that the clergy persuaded the young king to go on pilgrimage to the shrine of St. Duthac so that he could not attempt to save the Abbot of Fearn from the stake. It is certainly suggestive that Hamilton should have suffered on 29th February, and that James should be 'in the north country' in that month and had just returned from 'the extreme parts of his realm' a bare month after the 'reek' of Master Patrick Hamilton had begun to 'infect as many as it blew upon'. It is certain that James was in Tain at Easter 1534, when Ross Herald passed to London 'with writingis to the ambassatouris' and returned to St. Duthac's with answers to the King's grace; more than a year later a silver 'relic' of the saint, weighing 36 oz. and costing £5 to make and £7 to gild, was delivered to the king, and later 3s. was spent on two ells of canvas, presumably for wrapping it up.

By this time old William Spynie had gone to his rest, and Donald Munro (whose nephew and namesake wrote an account of the Western Isles) was provost of the collegiate kirk. The rapid line-up for that office — five presentees are named within just over three years — suggests unsettled times; the last of them (John Thornton) is on record in 1544 as enjoying a rather unhandy plurality by being also precentor of Moray. With his approval, Nicholas Ross feued the lands of his chaplainry of Dunskaith and the profits of the queen's ferry at Cromarty to his son Nicholas (recently legitimated), or to his three other natural sons in succession, and they might also build a 'sufficient house and other necessary policies'. About the same time, the chaplain of Newmore (John Bisset), with consent of the queen and the bishop, gave a feu charter of his church lands to a neighbouring laird.

Grave abuses were freely admitted to exist in the Scottish church at this time, but the difficulty was to find a method of removing them. The clergy who saw the writing on the wall would naturally be anxious to ensure that they and their families were not unprovided for, if the opportunities on which they had been able to count became closed to them. In this atmosphere of clerical immorality, plurality of offices, and appropriation of church lands, Nicholas Ross the younger was appointed provost of the collegiate church of Tain in March 1548/9, and the scene was set for the last decade of the old order and its final disappearance.

This is not the place to recount in detail the progress of

the Reformation in Scotland, but its impact on Tain can be gauged by three events which quickly followed each other in the year 1560. On 16th June, the queen regent's presentee to the vacant chaplainry of Newmore (a younger son of Munro of Foulis) was given possession through a procurator at the church in which it was founded 'by touching or delivery of the iron ring of the north door as also of the south door of said collegiate church'. Just a month later, Alexander Ross of Balnagown received from his 'speciale friend' Nicholas Ross, commendator of Fearn and provost of Tain, 'ane hede of silver callit sanct Duthois hede his chast blede [breast-bone] in gold and his ferthyr [case, or portable shrine] in silver gylt with gold', and bound himself under a penalty of 2,000 merks that these relics 'sal be furcht cumand to the said provost and college of Tayne and all uthers heffand entres [having interest] thairto by just titill'. One month later again, in mid-August, 'Nicholas of Ferne' sat among the representatives of the three estates of the realm in the 'Reformation Parliament' at Edinburgh, and voted with the majority (along with Robert Munro of Foulis) for accepting the reformed Confession of Faith, and forbidding the saying of mass and the exercise of all authority derived from Rome.

This brought to an end the activities for which the collegiate church existed. Its ceremonial ceased, and its relics, no longer venerated, were in the hands of strangers; but the structure survived, even if stripped of its finery, and the clergy were allowed to enjoy the fruits of their benefices, all but one-third which was to be devoted to augmenting the crown revenues and paying stipends to the Reformed clergy. The bishop of Ross (Henry Sinclair and his successor John Leslie the historian) adhered to the old church, but among those who went with the Reformers were the archdeacon, chancellor and treasurer of the diocese.

Many of the collegiate churches became parish churches, and presentations to prebends and chaplainries in some of them continued. An Act of 1567 ordained that patrons might grant such benefices as bursaries to students at the universities. Nicholas Ross retained the offices of provost and vicar of Tain until May 1567, and he died in September 1569; on his demission the parson of Alness, Thomas Ross, was appointed to hold the benefice and provostry as he would have done 'of auld before the alteratioun of the stait of religioun'. Up to 1587, when church lands were appropriated to the crown by Act of Parliament, the revenues of Newmore, Morangie, Tarlogie, Cambuscurrie and Dunskaith were granted regulary to boys for their support 'at the scule', and even for studies at Edinburgh and Cambridge.

And so, with more gradualness and less violence than is generally associated with the Reformation in Scotland, the old system of religious observance and ecclesiastical privilege changed its form or vanished entirely. But the town of Tain, which had grown up and found recognition under its shadow, remained and continued to develop.

4

Market Cross

BURGHS as we know them in Scotland today have an ancient origin, and the privileges of exclusive trade and commerce for which they came into existence reach back into the years before such matters were recorded in detail. Some of the earlier burghs still possess their foundation charters, however, or at least can point to authentic evidence of their granting; others have later charters which say specifically that they are renewing a right or confirming a position already granted by royal or noble authority; others again can show that they bore the burdens and responsibilities of burghal status before their rights to it can be established by anything stronger than tradition; while of some it must be presumed, in the absence of any proof to the contrary, that like Topsy they just 'growed'.

These varied origins are illustrated, to some extent at least, in the story of Tain and the other Ross-shire burghs. Dingwall had a charter of erection from Alexander II in 1226/7, according to a later confirmation; Cromarty makes its first appearance as a burgh in 1264; there are some grounds for placing the existence of Rosemarkie also as a burgh in the thirteenth century; but the latest expert opinion admits that Tain's origin as a burgh 'presents unanswerable questions'.[1] It is not denied, however, that its eminence as a sanctuary and place of pilgrimage dates from much earlier than any recorded reference to it as a burgh, and in fact it attracted to itself from an early date trading privileges comparable to those given to the great abbeys of the south.

Our only evidence for the trading rights conferred on the liberty or *immunitas* of Tain by Malcolm Canmore (who reigned from 1058 to 1093), and confirmed by his royal successors is the report of an inquiry or inquest which sat at Tain on 22nd April, 1439. Reference has already been made to their findings, but as the original document is missing, and there is no other bearing on this event, it is not now possible to learn the reason for holding such an inquiry. In the copy which has come down to us, this testimony regarding the ancient origin and trading privileges of Tain is said to bear the seal of Alexander Earl of Ross and Lord of the Isles, the king's justiciar north of the Forth; and the sederunt at Tain's first recorded meeting contains a formidable list of names, some recognisable as those of known individuals, and others which recur often in the history of Easter Ross.[2] Just three years earlier, for instance, the earl had appointed Alexander Mac-Culloch as his deputy with the title of 'Bailie of the Immunity of Tain', and this family held the office and the lands of Plaids for some 136 years, first under the earls and then direct from the king.

Tain's growing importance is reflected in another document, known through an official copy made from the original for the Lords of Council by the Clerk Register in 1564. It is a charter

1 *The Burghs of Scotland: a Critical List.* By the late Professor G. S. Pryde, revised by Professor A. A. M. Duncan (1965).

2 Translated from the Latin, the list reads: Alexander Sutherland master of Sutherland, William Leslie sheriff of Inverness, Hugh Ross of Balnagown, George Munro of Foulis, Alexander McCulloch, Alexander Henryson Sutherland, John Sutherland, William Caldor, William Terral, Hugh son of Alexander, George McCulloch, Hugh Munro younger, Donald son of Symon, Fercherd Reyid burgess of Inverness, John Moir of Calrossie, John Bayne, Donald McTyr, Donald the tailor ('sussorum'), John Spens, Andrew son of Alan, Andrew Tarrale, John Monylaw, Alexander Skynnane.

by the king himself, James II, dated at Inverness on 12th October, 1457; Tain must have been much in his mind just then, for only two days earlier he had endowed a chaplaincy in its parish church. It has been translated as follows:—

> Know that we for the praise and honour of God Omnipotent and of St. Duthac have approved ratified and by this our present charter have confirmed the infeftments donations and concessions made and granted in times past by our predecessors Kings of Scots to the said St. Duthac and to his collegiate church of Tain and those inhabiting the town itself with the immunity granted them within the four corner crosses placed around the limits of the bounds of Tain and all liberties and privileges whatsoever hitherto granted them by our said predecessors as freely quietly fully wholly honourably well and in peace as the chaplains clerics and inhabitants possessed and enjoyed the said immunity and liberties and privileges foresaid —

but he added a cautious rider that the confirmation must not prejudice the burgesses of Inverness or interfere with their privileges. There, of course, was the rub, for Inverness was the emporium of the Highlands; it had been a royal burgh for some 300 years, and had four charters from William the Lion conveying important and exclusive economic privileges over a wide area. The interests of the two were bound to clash, and in spite of the express reservation the people of Inverness seem to have taken alarm. They appealed to the king or his advisers to prevent any encroachment on their rights, and ten days later — after James had returned south — a royal letter made it abundantly clear that anything which Tain might gain was not to be at the expense of Inverness.

That this was more than a tiff between two burghs is shown by the fact that the Earl of Ross — grandson of that Donald of Harlaw who had given Inverness to the flames only 50 years before — seconded the royal wishes. He wrote in 1458 ordering his bailie of the girth of St. Duthac, John MacCulloch, and the inhabitants of Tain to help and defend their neighbours of

Inverness and to allow no impediment to be made to them in carrying on trade as authorised by the king.

The not unnatural jealousy shown by the magistrates of Inverness was to keep the northern towns at loggerheads for another century and a half, simply because privileges were granted to each which must lead to conflict. The trouble came to a head again at the end of 1493, when James IV was in Inverness a month after his first recorded visit to St. Duthac's shrine. He was told — and perhaps he may have seen for himself — that customable goods from Ross, Sutherland and Caithness which should have been brought before the royal customs officers and searchers at Inverness, and there paid the proper duties, had 'of long time byegone' gone instead 'to the burgh (*sic*) of Tain', where the duties had been collected by 'the bailies and community' and withheld by them to the prejudice of both the royal treasury and the burgh of Inverness.

The king and council determined that this should stop, or they would know the reason why. The people of Tain and the northern shires must in future bring their merchandise to the market of Inverness as their principal market, under the pain of forfeiting them, 'unto the time that they show if they have privileges or freedoms to the contrary of old'. It is not unlikely that the Inverness magistrates advised the king — as they were to do later with less reason — that Tain had no such authority to produce. Acting on this order, which was signed in the king's name on 12th November, the local sheriff made it known in Tain, probably by proclamation, in presence of Angus MacCulloch of Plaids and three bailies of the town.

Any effect this may have had was apparently short-lived, for the burgh of Inverness maintained vigorous legal proceedings between 1499 and 1501 against Tain, and also against Dingwall. Fourteen inhabitants of Tain were summoned to appear before the king and his council at Inverness, and after several hearings, the Tain men were ordered to desist from the trading objected to, unless they could produce their authority. In July 1501, the council continued the case with the consent of both parties 'in the hope of concord' till the next justice aire at Elgin.

That is the last we hear of the dispute for some time, but the 'greit enormytie and trespass' which had grown up in the remoter parts of the wide sheriffdom of Inverness was one of the reasons for an Act of Parliament in March 1503/4 creating a separate Sheriff of Ross — to sit 'in Thane or Dinguale' according to the case to be dealt with — and a Sheriff of Caithness to sit at Dornoch or Wick.

These proceedings throw some light on Tain's early trade and traders. Skins, hides, salmon, iron and other merchandise are all mentioned — one of the sites of old iron workings is near Edderton, where bog iron is found. In the mid-sixteenth century 'casualties' were payable to the hereditary bailie for the brewing of ale, peats, beef and fish; among the crops were oats and bere and stock included sheep and capons. Sugar and spices, as well as coats of mail and cannon, were being imported through Cromarty.

The names of the Tain men alleged to have been buying and selling are Alexander (or David) Dean, James Tulloch, Donald MacCulloch, John Davidson, Hugh Alexanderson, George Munro, Donald Paterson (Patrickson), ———— Laurenceson, Magnus Faed, Steven Fudes (Fyddes), Donald Brabner, Andrew Forres, Cristy Chapman, Alexander Smyth, and 'ane called Gillaspy'. Fifteen years later, Alexander Smyth and another from Tain are charged with helping three Dundee burgesses to buy salmon and grilse and ship them without paying customs.

Tain was now achieving some corporate existence, no longer wholly ecclesiastical. A charter of 1484 witnessed by Thomas Monelaw, which has already been mentioned, was granted by a number of 'common citizens and clerks of the town of the kind confessor blessed St. Duthac of Tayne with other common citizens and clerks of our community'. They include several neighbouring lairds and a number of people known only by patronymic, as follows:— John Ross of Balnagown, John Munro of Foulis, Masters Donald and William Ross, Angus MacCulloch of Plaids, William Maktyre of Innerathie, Angus MacCulloch of Tarrell, John Wauss of Lochslyn, John Mercall of Dawachcartye, Finlay and John

Faid, Patrick son of John, Stephen Foress, William Clark, Donald Red son of Tormot, Donald Red son of Michael, John Makaryne, John son of Patrick, Finlay McCarryn, John son of Donald, David Broug, Donald Maktyre, William Pedison, John Red, Donald Talzour, Robert Tulloch, Patrick Fores, Finlay Makbei, Donald McFersoun and Thomas McFerson.

This group of people, using 'our seal' (which from a document of about the same time was 'the common seal of the said toun of Tayne') granted a piece of land in the town to the Subdean of Ross (Thomas Ross), and later sasine was given by Patrick Johnstoun 'our bailie'. The word 'burgh' is not used, and the earliest extant charter granting that status was still a century ahead, but we are now coming to a time when the designation creeps even into the most formal documents, and when Tain was assuming the responsibilities of such a status. The first royal document in which Tain is called a burgh that has yet come to light is the letter sent in the king's name after a privy council meeting at Inverness in November 1493 (although the 1499/1501 series of letters studiously refer to the 'town' of Tain as distinct from the 'burgh' of Inverness); it figures as a burgh in the Acts of the Lords Auditors in 1494 and 1496; it appears in a list of burghs and bounds whose customs were granted to the captain of Stirling Castle under a privy seal letter in 1505, and in a list of 1524 of certain northern burghs in which the Abbot of Arbroath possessed rights.

Applying the test of when Tain began to pay its share of the burdens rather than claim or even be accorded burghal status, we find it making a contribution in 1532/3 for conveying the king's artillery to the Border. Its name is on the earliest stent roll of the Convention of Royal Burghs in 1535, when it paid taxes twice — once for the king's journey to France for a bride, and once for the defence of the Borders. Its commissioners occasionally attended meetings of the Convention (*e.g.*, Andro Rysie in 1581, Finlay Manson in 1586), and in 1567 it was even represented in Parliament, although the records do not say by whom. But when we learn that Arbroath (for example) was stented more than a century before becoming a royal burgh, and was in Parliament twenty years before receiving a formal charter, it is plain that there were many anomalies in practice, even though burghs had enjoyed a formally recognised status as early as the mid-twelfth century.

The use of the terms 'provost' and 'bailies' has sometimes been thought to indicate the existence of a burgh, but a statement by Nicholas Ross which has been preserved is evidence to the contrary. He 'answers peremptorily' to the pretended summons and charge pursued against him 'by the alleged bailies and community of the town of Tayne', who had asked — no doubt in the immediately post-Reformation period — that the seal and charters should be handed over to them. In the preamble to his reasons for refusing, he probably would not seek to minimise the importance of himself and his office:—

'. . . I am, as I have been these diverse years last bypast, undoubted provost of the College Kirk of Tayne, and I and my predecessors provosts thereof by reason of the said provostry were also provosts of the said town, so reputed and held past memories of man, and the whole courts of the same during the space foresaid fenced in my predecessors' names as provosts thereof, and the bailies of the said town yearly during the same space chosen and elected by me and my predecessors provosts foresaids, and the whole escheats of the court of the said town by erection and foundation appertaining to the said provost, and seeing I and my predecessors not only are provosts of the said Kirk but also provosts of the said town and principal persons thereof. . .'

As well as the town's bailies, of whom two or even three are on record together, there was also — and remained down to the Forty-Five — a heritable bailie of the immunity of Tain, already mentioned more than once. This office had been granted in 1436 to the MacCullochs of Plaids by the Earl of Ross (who reserved the escheats to himself, and in fact once describes himself as 'aldermannus' of Tain); after the earldom was forfeited the grant was renewed by the king. In 1552

Robert MacCulloch of Plaids sold the lands and office to his uncle, Alexander Innes of Cadboll, who was charged by an order from Queen Mary and her consort to hold courts within the town and immunity as often as necessary. By an agreement reached with Nicholas Ross in 1566, the escheats of the court were to go two parts to the 'utility and profit of the said provost', and the third part to the bailie 'for service and execution of office'. Having passed to Innes of that Ilk, the bailiary was sold by him in 1584 to George Sinclair of Mey, in Caithness, whose son William married a daughter of Balnagown. The office of bailie — which simply signifies deputy — may well have been profitable to the holder, to judge from lists of the 'casualties' levied.

It is plain from all this that Tain was becoming a place of increasing importance for trade. This gave rise to further jealousy, and in 1580 Inverness complained to the Convention of Royal Burghs against eight towns in the North for usurping its trading rights. The Convention found that Dingwall, Chanonry, Rosemarkie, Cromarty, Dornoch and Wick, since they were not enrolled and paid no stent, 'are nocht in the societie of the remanent frie burrowis'; Tain alone of the group was ordered to appear at the next meeting to exhibit the right, charter and privilege whereby it was erected into a free burgh — 'gif they ony have', adds the minute menacingly. Failing to appear, Tain was fined for non-attendance (Inverness cannily objecting to such an implied recognition of status), and the dispute dragged on. In 1582 the privy council, harking back to their decision of 1501, again charged the people of Tain to stop buying skins, hides, iron, salmon and other merchandise, 'aye and until' they showed any proper authority for doing so.

Not long after this impasse had been reached, Tain received its oldest extant charter, in which its claims were freely acknowledged in the formal language of such documents. It is of interest also as one of the early grants by James VI when he took control of affairs on reaching the age of 21 after a stormy minority, only a little more than four months after his mother's execution. As part of the young king's means of ensuring an independent revenue, Parliament in July 1587 passed three Acts — one in which he revoked all grants made to the prejudice of the crown during his mother's reign and his own minority; another which annexed to the crown the lands belonging to the prelates, the abbeys and monasteries, the 'college kirks' and other similar establishments; and a third which empowered the king to grant lands in the earldom of Ross.

Six months later, at Holyrood House on 10th January, 1587/8, a charter by King James in favour of the Royal Burgh of Tain passed the great seal. It mentioned the destruction of its muniments, 'by barbarians and certain rebellious Ersch subjects, as is contained in authentic testimonies produced before us'; the privileges granted to it by former kings as a 'free royal burgh'; and the discharge of its obligation to attend Parliament, Convention of Estates, and Convention of Royal Burghs, and contribution to the burghs' taxes; and accordingly the king ratified, confirmed and renewed its ancient privileges, infeftments and rights in the broadest terms. These included the holding of land (to be perambulated yearly), the privilege of free markets, the power to elect provost, bailies, dean of guild, treasurer, councillors and officers, and the right to import and sell goods and collect and receive petty customs — all 'as if the infeftments of the burgh had not been destroyed and burnt'.

By ordering that the burgh's weekly market, hitherto held on the Lord's Day, should for all time to come be held 'on the Sabbath Day called Setterday', the charter sheds an interesting light on Sunday observance in King James's day, and incidentally proves that Tain already had an established weekly market. It also authorised and named a series of yearly markets.

Tain was the second of the Northern burghs to have its status confirmed or acknowledged by King James. Dingwall was the first (1587), and Wick followed in 1589, Chanonry in 1590, Inverness and Rosemarkie in 1592, and Cromarty in 1593. Dornoch did not become a royal burgh until 1628.

5

Regent Moray pulpit

BESIDES the Church and the Burgh, there is a third strand in the history of Tain made up of the families and clans, great and small, which lived within the four girth crosses and beyond. No town, especially in those days, could live only to itself; and it would be a false picture of the burgh which left out of account the surrounding district and the neighbours who lived in it. Principal among them were the Rosses, and their band of followers and allies bearing such names as MacCulloch, Denoon, Vass, Tarrell, Corbett, Fearn, Mactyre and Faid.

The Rosses of Balnagown, chiefs of the name, were descended from Hugh, the younger son of the fourth earl of the older line. Hugh held lands on both sides of Tain, for he was given Rarichies beyond Fearn by his father (killed at Halidonhill in 1333) and Balnagown and others by his brother Earl William. His sister married King Robert II, who confirmed these lands to his son William in 1374 and 1376. In the next generation Walter of Balnagown married Catherine, daughter and heiress of Paul McTyre, who is said to have brought him more lands to the north; their grandson Alexander fell in a bloody fight with the Mackays in 1487, when 'seventeen other landed gentlemen of the province of Ross' — including Rosses, Tarrells and Vasses — were slain with him in Strathcarron.

It was in Tain that this chief's grandson, Walter Ross of Balnagown, was killed some forty years later, but written sources have no more to say about what happened; perhaps, like his younger brother William, he was buried 'in the parish church of Tane at the south side of Our Lady altar'. His son Alexander probably succeeded as a young man, and before the battle of Pinkie he paid an £80 penalty for not joining the royal army with his clan; it was he, as Laird of Balnagown at the Reformation, who received from his kinsman Nicholas (the Provost) the relics of St. Duthac for safe keeping. But Alexander is remembered as a lawless chief who feared neither God nor the king, and he even laid waste the 'battelit tour' of Plaids on Tain's doorstep. In 1577 his heir, kinsmen and friends, meeting in Tain, went the length of petitioning him to avoid any further folly, by which he might 'tyne the riggis [lose the lands] that his elders wan'. After a spell inside the walls of Tantallon, letters of fire and sword were issued against him in 1583, and his son George was actually charged to 'convocat the lieges' and pursue him.

Such, then, was Tain's most powerful neighbour when it received King James's charter in 1588. By the 'General Band' enacted in the previous year, Balnagown was one of the Highland chiefs made responsible for the orderly conduct not only of his own clan but also of any 'broken men' living on his lands. A similar duty was laid on his neighbour to the west, Robert Munro of Foulis, whose clan occupied a narrow wedge of country running from the Cromarty Firth far into the hills. The Laird of Foulis is heard of fairly often in the story of Tain, and it so happens that Robert *mor* (who had been chief since his father fell at Pinkie forty years before) was soon to be succeeded by Mr Hector, who as a younger son had been bred to the Church. He was, in fact, the same young man who was admitted to a chaplaincy in the collegiate church on the eve of the Reformation; since then he had risen to be Dean of Ross — but his closest association with Tain was a strange one, for he and his mother (of the Balnagown family) had got mixed up with a coven of witches from the town, and a bailie and four burgesses of Tain served on the jury which heard all about the unholy rites in which they were said to have taken part. The evidence consisted almost entirely of confessions wrung from the witches themselves, however, and mother and son were acquitted.

But such great folk were not Tain's only neighbours, and a glance around the farmlands of Easter Ross will afford a few other examples. First among the lesser landed families who made their impact on Tain in those days were the innumerable MacCullochs: chartered in Plaids by the Earl of Ross in 1436, and established in one estate or another (latterly Kindeace and Glastullich) for more than a dozen generations, they absorbed an even older Easter Ross family, the Tarrells, and much of the property which they acquired passed later — through Inneses, Sinclairs or Munros — to the Mackenzies, when they 'leap-frogged' eastwards over the Munros and Rosses. Three other families, whose lands went at least in part to swell the Mackenzie holdings, were the Corbetts, who had Easter Ard from the earl in 1463, and were later in Arboll; the Vasses of Lochslin, who held by royal charter (renewed in 1512) and built a castle of which the ruins still stand; and the Dunbars of Tarbat, who had a charter from James V, one of whom married a Corbett and another handed over to Monro of Tarrell.

Then there were smaller families still, who had a bit here and a bit there; and smaller estates too, with a bewildering succession of owners. There were Denoons in part of Arboll, Pittogartie, Pitnelies and Cadboll; and an estate like Invereathie had a succession of Mactyres, Vasses, Faids and Urquharts, most of them related by marriage and no doubt some sharing the lands among them.

This roll of the ancient names of Easter Ross, many of which survive there today as well as being scattered across the world, introduces a period when family loyalties were often tested, and a man's enemies might be those of his own household. New names were coming in, as well as old ones disappearing. Sir William Keith, a courtier who had been much in the young king's confidence, and held the post of Master of the Wardrobe, had a charter in 1587 as 'heritable feuar' of the barony of Delny (and later that of Dingwall also) and as bailie principal of the earldom of Ross. As an incomer he may not have been too popular, and he complained bitterly to the king when his depute (John Vass of Lochslin) and his own brother were interrupted by 400 armed men — a burgess and several inhabitants of Tain among them — while trying to hold a bailie court within the barony, and compelled by their insolent behaviour and 'contumelious speeches' to bring the prosecution of justice to an undignified end.

Sir William did not last long as a Ross-shire baron (Delny went to his brother John in 1594, and it later drifted to the Mackenzies through Lord Balmerino and Sir Robert Innes of that Ilk), but he deserves more than passing notice as the first Provost of the Royal Burgh of Tain of whom there is any record, as distinct from the provost of the collegiate church whose office had now ceased to exist. As no burgh records have survived from the first seventy years or more after the 1588 charter, we know next to nothing of his election or conduct as provost. Several Acts of Parliament laid it down that only resident merchants could be magistrates of burghs, but these were more honoured in the breach than the observance. Sir William was chosen for the post, more than likely, as a known favourite of the king who had granted the burgh's charter: any democratic procedure is discounted by the high-handed way in which Alexander Ross of Balnagown appeared before the bailies in November 1588 and produced a commission from 'Sir Wm. Keyth of Delnye provest of Tayne' demitting that office in favour of Balnagown, who accordingly required to be admitted to it. An extract from the burgh books by William Fraser, clerk *pro tempore*, solemnly records that 'the balleis, consell and haill communitie uananimiter hes votit and consentit . . . and hes ressavit his aith of fidelitie'. The only other surviving record of Sir William's term of office shows that a missive from Tain to the Convention of Burghs was signed only by him as provost, and therefore insufficiently vouched; but they were let off the appropriate fine 'in respect of their poverty'.

The Convention, in whose minutes a commissioner for Tain intermittently appears, met by royal authority 'to treat upon the welfare of merchants, merchandise, good rule and statutes for the common profit of the burghs'. They generally chose Edinburgh for their meetings, but they also met in Aberdeen, Perth, Stirling and other places. The burghs paid their share of national taxation, and sundry other payments, loans and gifts to the king were carried through by the Convention. When the Privy Council asked them to fit out and furnish six ships to convoy the king and his Danish bride home in 1590, for example, Tain was named as one of ten burghs to help Aberdeen in fitting out one of them. (It was probably only a coincidence that the late provost of the only burgh north of Inverness called on to participate had sailed with the king on this expedition as a member of his household).

It is a curious commentary on central and local government in those days that Balnagown, just three months before he was admitted Provost, was being accused of grave matters by the local presbytery, the commissioner appointed by the general assembly to oversee the kirks of Ross, and the Church's legal adviser. According to them, he had made the chapterhouse of the old collegiate church a girnel and larder and put it to 'other profane uses' which prevented the commissioner and brethren from meeting there. Not only this, but his clansman John Ross of Little Allan was said to have taken over the nearby 'hous of auld dedicat for a scuilhous . . . maist necessar for upbringing of the youth in edificiatioun and gude letteris', thus leaving the local youth without accommodation and 'greitlie frustrat of learning'. The Privy Council, when appealed to, curtly ordered the offenders to 'red thameselfis guids and geir' from both 'chaptor' and schoolhouse, so that they might be used for their proper purposes.

Most of the references to the Church in and about Tain during the decades following the Reformation make dismal reading. The old religion had brought celebrity to the town, and no doubt worldly gain as well; but the ornately-carved oaken pulpit which adorned what was left of the collegiate church was — according to tradition — given by the Regent Moray in testimony of the people's zeal in the Reformation cause. But it cannot have been easy to find ministers fitted for the northern parishes, and even Balnagown himself had to be forced by law to disgorge the teinds which were the chief source of the ministers' sustenance. Before the Reformation the collegiate church had been often put to secular uses — in a land transaction of 1495 the parties swore an oath to observe its terms on St. Duthac's altar — and now it was not unexpected to find a document providing for payment of money 'betwix the sone rysing and down passing of the samyn within the paroche kirk of Tayne at ony patent or convenient place thairin'.

Besides plain irreligion, there was rank superstition. Mention has already been made of the activities of witches from Tain: the report in Pitcairn's *Criminal Trials* of the case involving the Munros of Foulis says that Christian Ross, who entertained one of the stars of the coven named Marion Ross (*alias* 'Loske Loncart') at her home in Tain, and William Mac-Gillivray who bought poison in Tain were convicted and burnt, probably at Chanonry, in 1577. The same year as that in which Lady Foulis and her son were found 'not guilty' brought a spectacular but more harmless visitation: 'In the ewening George Dunbar in Thane sa and mony may with him ane battell abue them upone ane hill callit Knokbane quhilk did last twa owris and vanist away. It is alegit that it wes the sche wycthis' (she witches).

As so often happens, it probably took a hint of persecution and interference with spiritual liberty to awaken the Church in the North. John Munro, a nephew of Robert *mor* of Foulis, became minister of Tain and Subdean of Ross in 1599, when King James was preparing the way for a return to episcopacy by curbing the powers of the general assembly. Those who held to the Kirk's supremacy in spiritual affairs would not concede the king's right to determine when and where the assembly should meet, and the test came when he announced that one fixed to be held at Aberdeen in 1604 was to be postponed. In July 1605, Andrew Melville and the extreme presbyterian party decided to risk a charge of treason by themselves constituting an assembly: one of the nineteen ministers taking part — and one of the three on the leet chosen for moderator — was John Munro, representing the Presbytery of Tain. To James the proceedings savoured of 'nothing else but of sedition and plain contempt of us and our authority'. Summoned before the Privy Council, some submitted; but the minister of Tain refused, and was sentenced to banishment in Kintyre. He escaped with another minister while imprisoned in Doune Castle, was declared rebel for absenting himself while awaiting judgment from the Privy Council in 1607, and coolly returned to his ministry in Tain. He must have been well supported, for he was still there three years later when the Privy Council sent this stern reminder of the duties of a royal burgh to their 'right traiste freindis, the Provost and Baillies of Tayne':—

'. . . we mervell not a little, that you, who are his Majestie's officers, armed with his Majestie's Royal power and auctoritie, sould by your connivance, suffer anie such persenis, who standis under his Majestie's offence, hef so peaceable a residence and free exercese of their calling amang you, seeing in dewitie of your offices you stand answerable to his Majestie for every such errour and oversight, wherewith in reason you may be burdennit; and thairfor chairges are direct againis you for the apprehensionn of the said Mr Johnne, and keeping of him prisonner in some chalmer of yeur toune quhil he purge himself of his rebellioun . . .'

But this gesture of independence, in which both presbytery and town council seem to have connived (the provost was John's brother, Hector Munro of Assynt, and the presbyters included several others of the clan), could not halt the king's policy. Presbyteries had by this time been saddled with 'constant moderators' (Tain had John Ross of Little Tarrel,

49

minister of Kilmuir Wester), and the bishops were back with many of their old powers. During these exciting times the kirk of Tain seems to have been allowed to fall into a bad state through neglect, for in 1612 the large sum of £227 was raised among the citizens for its repair.

This is a reminder of the new responsibilities which had been assumed under the burgh's charter, and also of the fact that annexation of church lands meant that funds for such purposes must be found elsewhere. Possessions in the form of lands and rights to mills, fishings, grazings, tolls and customs formed a property held in trust by the community to enable the burgh to discharge its local and national obligations. Certain sums payable before 1588 to the clerics of St. Duthac's church now went to 'the common good of the burgh of Tayne', and from 1608 court fines were shared by the burgh and the hereditary bailie (an office by this time bought with the lands of Plaids by Sinclair of Mey). References to little parcels of land, tenements and biggings, each carefully located in relation to its neighbours, fill the burgh documents of the early seventeenth century, and terms such as the common lands, loanings, braes, moor and green, as well as the common way, make their appearance.

Trade came to take a more important place in the community as Tain's eminence as a resort of pilgrims faded. The inhabitants now included merchants of various kinds, dyers, tailors, shoemakers and maltmen — most if not all of them also holding some arable land and spending part of their time farming and raising crops. A list of sums owed to the widow of a Tain burgess in 1613 shows that the privilege of trading within the burgh was worth having, for the customers included the lairds of Balnagown and Foulis, Mackay of Scourie, and many more. The boot was now on the other foot, and Tain complained to the convention against Inverness for allowing 'unfree trafficqueris and unfreemen' dwelling at the Kirkton of Alness to trade and taking money from them.

There were increasing signs that the markets authorised by the 1588 charter were attracting buyers and sellers from a wide area and even from the far north, to the benefit of the town's finances. The burgh had its own mills at Aldie, let at 50s. a year, with a number of tenants bound to take their grain there and nowhere else for grinding; this right was confirmed by royal charter in 1609. Perhaps in the hope of adding to its seaborne trade, Tain was one of three burghs which in 1604 craved the convention's support for repair of their 'harbour and shore', as they were ruinous and 'habill to decay'.

King James was now far away in London, but he stuck to his belief in 'plantation' or 'settlement' as a means of pacifying and civilising the backward parts of his kingdom, and also looked to the royal burghs as a source of revenue to the crown. The founding of Stornoway was a result of this policy, and it also seems that a few families from the shores of the Firth of Forth were encouraged to settle at Cromarty to develop the fisheries. This suggests that it was more than a meaningless formula that was written into the preamble to Tain's next charter, in which its rights as a royal burgh were renewed by King James in 1612 on the advice of the Receiver-General of Customs and Casualties in Scotland (Sir John Arnot) and the Privy Council in general:—

'. . . considering the necessity of the burgh not only for the reception convenience and welfare of the inhabitants of the islands and highlands of our Kingdom of Scotland and others repairing to and frequenting the burgh for the education and instruction of the youths and children thereof in virtue civility and learning but also for the increase of orderly government (*policia*) and public works within the said burgh . . .'

Besides confirming all earlier grants, including the right to hold a weekly market and five annual fairs, the charter contains three items which are either more specific than before or actually new. It is the first Tain charter where lands are named inside and outside the burgh to which it is given rights[1]; the grant of all mussel scalps within sight of the

1 '. . . lands and grazings called Badis and Raaniche possessed and perambulated yearly within the four corner crosses called girth crosses lying round our said burgh . . . lands of Innerathie lands of Gortinges Clerk Island and Priest Island with the pertinents of the same pertaining to the burgh as proper parts of the common lands of the said burgh so possessed and enjoyed beyond the memory of man; . . .'

burgh lands, including one named 'St. Duthac's Scalp', provides an important and unusual source of burgh revenue[1]; and the right to 'daill silver', or money given as dole or alms, of any chapels, altars, prebends etc. within the burgh is one of several such recorded post-Reformation grants.

The charter was dated at Edinburgh on 3rd November, about ten days after Parliament had ratified Tain's infeftments in general terms. On that occasion Inverness protested, and some years later (in 1641) uplifting the small customs of Tain and other northern burghs was still being included among the rights and privileges of Inverness.

Considerable trade was then being carried on between Scotland's northern ports and those of Holland and France, and the records of the day confirm that Tain had its share. The chief grain grown in Ross was bere, a species of early ripening barley suited to rough farming, and a report for 1620/21 by John Dougall — presumably one of Sir John Arnot's men — shows that in twelve months as much as 206 chalders of bere were exported from ports north of the Spey, with fairly large quantities of hides, beef and salmon. Findhorn, Inverness, Dingwall, Cromarty and harbours in Caithness took part in the trade; the only two Tain items reported are a cargo of 12 chalders of bere belonging to an Edinburgh merchant sent 'out of Taine to Holland in Peter Wilsones bark of Leith callit the Harpe', and 20 chalders (of which a Tain burgess was half owner) from Sutherland to Holland in an Aberdeen ship. In the same period some 640 hides — of oxen, kye and harts — were shipped to France or Holland from Findhorn or Caithness, and there is evidence that Tain had an interest in this trade too, at any rate for home use. Lord Erskine, son of King James's Treasurer the Earl of Mar, had been given a monopoly of the leather trade to enable him to reform Scottish tanning practice, and in 1622 most of the chief gentry met his commissioners at Tain and promised to come with all their men, tenants and servants east of the bridge of Alness to offer their 'haill leather' to be 'tannit,

1   In the same year Parliament granted to the burgh of St. Andrews the 'mussil scap' near Pilmuir at the mouth of the River Eden, and this was confirmed by the king in 1620.

barkit, dryit, and stampitt' by twelve local tanners and rede-
livered to the owners.

A trading rival to the north testified that 'this whyle bypast
all the merchandise and trafick of Strathnawer and Sutherland hath bein transported ower to Tayne, wherebye it is
enriched and Dornoch depauperat'. It was probably due to
the same writer — the wily old Tutor of Sutherland, Sir Robert
Gordon of Gordonstoun — that Dornoch was made a royal
burgh in 1628, for he strongly advised his nephew on entering
upon his estate to 'mack strait and seweir acts in your courts
that no merchandise be transported ower into Tayne, except
it be first brought to the towne of Dornoch and offered to be
sold ther.'

In spite of this, however, there are signs that Tain's finances
were genuinely distressed. Permission to miss three con-
ventions was given in 1628, so long as expenses that would
have been paid to the burgh's commissioner were spent on
'common works' (which generally meant repairs to tolbooth,
church or harbour). That Tain was not simply pleading poverty
in order to avoid taxation is shown by a return made to the
Exchequer of the burgh's Common Good for 1634[1]:—

Charge

Item first chairges thame selffis for the common girss and brayis of the said burghe, being roupit extends to	40 lib.
Item the customes of the tua frie fairis of the said burghe being roupit extendis to	50 lib.
Item for the toll and pittie customes of the said burghe extendis to	20 lib.

Discharge   Summa 110 lib.

Item to the Clerk in his fie	40 lib.
Item to the Reider yeirlie	100 lib.
Item to the Maister of the Gramour and Musick schools	100 lib.

Summa 240 lib.

and so super expendit be 130 lib.

1   In the same year Cromarty out of a Common Good of 40 lib. 'super expended' £16 6s.
8d., while in 1671 Dingwall declared that it had no common good except £20 Scots yearly
which it paid to the common clerk for his fee.

Finance, however, was plainly not the only measure of a burgh's importance. Tain had had two charters from the king who sat in London, and its own representative sat in the Scots Parliament which received a royal harangue during his Majesty's salmon-like return to his native land in 1617. The provost and bailies of Tain were included for the first time in a commission from the Privy Council to apprehend a bunch of cattle thieves, and about the same time an Aberdeen burgess called on them to prosecute the contraveners of his monopoly to fish for pearls in northern waters.

There were also occasions when Tain needed to put its own house in order. One day in May 1619, a Ross clansman in the town 'on lawful business' was persuaded on some pretext to go to the Angel Hill, 'quhilk is the ordinair place of execution', where a notary named Angus Williamson and his accomplices disarmed him and stole his purse with 100 merks of silver, beat him up, and left him for dead after dragging him by the hair of the head down the brae to an out-of-the-way spot. While St. Barquhan's Fair was being held in 1622, a tenant of Sir Donald Mackay's from Strathnaver was attacked by Donald MacLeod of Assynt and his four sons at the market cross, and they took a number of horses off him by dressing up one of the company with his Majesty's 'blasin and armes upoun his breast' and producing counterfeit letters of arrestment. In neither of these cases — although the King's Advocate took notice of the misuse of the royal arms — is there any word of the perpetrators being brought to book.

Courts sat for the administration of justice and the arrangement of public affairs in the old tolbooth of Tain, which was also a prison for those who were caught. But the burgh now considered itself important enough — and not too poor — to build a 'steeple' with bartizans, and to send to Flanders for a town bell. Cast by a master founder of Middelburg, whose father had made one for Whithorn twenty years earlier, the bell carried on its rim an inscription which said reverently—

ANNO . 1630 . SOLI . DEO . GLORIA . MICHAEL . BURGERHUS . ME . FECIT

Two inscribed stones on the tower were more worldly:

THIS WARK
BIGIT 1631
JHON MACKULLOCH
BEING PROVOST

. . . .
BAILZIES

Today, from another tower, the original bell still rings the nightly curfew — but the old steeple collapsed after standing insecurely through the decades of turmoil which followed its building.

6

"The Ark"

To anyone who tries to understand the reasons behind men's actions, the period of the civil war from 1639 to 1651 is likely to be confusing. It must have seemed equally confused to the people of Easter Ross, who often encountered the contending armies although far from the centre of affairs.

The primary cause of the outbreak was religious. James VI had re-established the bishops without too much opposition, but there was serious trouble when Charles I tried to impose on the Scots a liturgy similar to the prayer book of the Church of England. Assembly and Parliament replied with the National Covenant of 1638, of which every burgh and parish was to have a copy, and for which signatures were collected up and down the country. Intended primarily for the defence of religion, the Covenant included an assertion of parliamentary authority. The king would have none of it, and the Covenanters began to raise men — for the first time this was not simply a magnates' levy, but an army of mercenary officers and local recruits; the burghs were called on to provide money to pay and maintain them, and the citizens had also to help in quartering and feeding the troops when the course of a campaign brought the army to their doors.

To clarify the impact of the civil war on Tain and Easter Ross, its general course may be divided into several phases, sometimes rather arbitrary, as follows:— The Bishops' Wars ended in the Scots' favour, their demands of Charles being met, and after the outbreak of civil war in England there was a realignment of parties with Montrose and some other former Covenanters supporting the king (1639/43); the Solemn League and Covenant brought an alliance with the English Parliament against the king, the '*annus mirabilis*' of Montrose's campaign, his defeat and the flight of Charles to the Scots to escape the English (1643/46); Charles's later imprisonment by the English army caused a split in the ranks of the Covenanters, with two-thirds of Parliament supporting Hamilton's 'Engagement' to rescue the king but after Hamilton's defeat at Preston, Argyll and the extremists took over and allied with Cromwell (1647/48); following the king's execution, many moderates would have supported Charles II if he had taken the Covenant, but he delayed negotiations in the hope that Montrose would win his second campaign (1649/50); Charles took the Covenant and was crowned, Scotland united under him against Cromwell but suffered defeat at Inverkeithing and Worcester (1650/51); finally, with Cromwell in charge and Scotland an occupied country, Glencairn's and Middleton's risings were defeated (1653/54).

For most of this time, it is worth remembering, there was a sort of 'floating vote' between ultra-royalist and ultra-Covenanter. Local loyalties might play a part in the decision whom to support: in Easter Ross, for example, the general balance of sympathy usually found the Rosses and Munros (whose chief was a minor up to 1651) on the 'kirk' side and against the Mackenzies, except when the Covenanters became too anti-royal.

Tain played its part at the centre of affairs when the National

Covenant was adopted. Its parish minister, Gilbert Murray, represented the presbytery at the Glasgow Assembly of 1638, and the name of the burgh's commissioner to Parliament, Thomas McCulloch, can still be read in the compartment allotted to Tain in the margin of a splendid copy of the Covenant dated 1639[1]. The Earl of Sutherland was the leading Covenanter in the North, and we find the Provost of Tain acting under him along with some of the local lairds, while a cash levy was made on the burgh by Parliament. Although David Ross of Balnagown probably had some influence over his clansmen in and about Tain, as well as those on his own estates, the men of Easter Ross made no great showing in the Bishops' War, and of actual fighting the district saw none. But there were signs and portents in plenty, and Highlanders interpreted variously the 'apparitions, spectraes, strange sights, which presaged warr and revolutions, such as men fighting in the aire, horse and foot, retreating, returning again . . .'

So the spring of 1644 brought news that Montrose was coming North as the king's lieutenant-general. Argyll was in Strathbogie, and from Dunrobin Sutherland called on Balnagown, the Tutor of Foulis and others to meet him at Tain. That summer Sutherland and Seaforth, with the Rosses, Munros and others marched to Strathspey, but they were denied a fight by Montrose's ally Alexander Macdonald (Colkitto).

Tain had the thrill of watching Thomas Fraser of Strichen, Sheriff-Principal of Inverness-shire, coming 'in progress' with the barons and gentry of Ross to receive two notable prisoners, the Marquess of Huntly and the Laird of Drum, who had fled to Strathnaver and were now being convoyed south. Sutherland and Balnagown joined the sheriff's escort, and the earl put the strength of his own forces at 1,600 foot ('as for horses', he added ruefully, 'the Parliament did consider we wer unable to furnish anie, and therfor did dispence with them.').

In January 1645 some men from Tain may have been in the

1   Original in National Library of Scotland; reproduced in J. K. Hewison, *The Covenanters*, vol. I.

'rabble of new levies, peasants, drovers, shopmen, servants, and camp-followers' who made their way as far as the south end of Loch Ness to oppose Montrose — only to be left in the air when he doubled back in his famous surprise march through the hills to victory over Argyll at Inverlochy; and again in May, when a force under General Hurry was beaten by Montrose at Auldearn near Nairn. But the brilliant run of successes was broken at Philiphaugh and an ardent royalist reported 'the King's cause weak, the Covenanters carry all. . . . Ross, Sutherland and Caithness complying with the government in church and state'. Garrisons were planted in the North, with one even 'in the Castle of Braan uppon Seaforts nose'.

With the king in English hands, the 'Engagement' was supported by a section of the Scots leaders, but the Assembly condemned it and most of the ministers did all in their power to obstruct recruiting. Some at least of the Rosses and Munros entered into it, but one of its chief supporters in the North accused the magistrates of Tain of 'not putting out their men to the last engadgment'. This was Colonel Hugh Rose of Kilravock, Sheriff of Inverness, who was in Tain in September 1648 with 100 foot and 35 horse, which he proceeded to quarter on the burgh for four days and four nights. Neither Kilravock nor his officers would pay a penny in return, the townsmen complained, although the grass and corn were maliciously destroyed. When he produced a warrant for three months' maintenance for his troops the magistrates at first refused to acknowledge it without an order from the committee of estates in Parliament; but on the advice of Sinclair of Mey and Sutherland of Dunbeath they granted a bond, which Parliament later cancelled. On the provost's supplication, the burgh's monthly payment was twice reduced, in 1647 and 1649, seeing that Tain remained in a distressed condition.

An important non-military act of this period was the disjunction of the shire of Ross from Inverness, to which it had continued to be tied in spite of the Act passed in 1504. David Ross of Balnagown and Sir Robert Innes of that Ilk, for themselves and in name of the freeholders and inhabitants, pointed out that Caithness and Sutherland had already been disjoined under the old Act, but for the people of Ross justice was often frustrated by the 36 miles and two ferries which separated them from Inverness: in the smallest storm they simply could not get there. Accordingly on 16th March 1649 Parliament ratified the 1504 Act and disjoined the Sheriffdom of Ross, appointing Tain to be the head burgh thereof (the petitioners had asked that Tain and Dingwall should both, as laid down in 1504, be places where the sheriff would sit for the administration of justice, as he found expedient). Argyll was made Sheriff of Ross as well as of Inverness, but he was soon succeeded by Robert Munro of Obsdale (later Sir Robert of Foulis).

In January 1649, a few days before the king's execution, the Scots Parliament passed an Act excluding all 'Engagers' and their sympathisers from public office. Some men from Tain may have been among the Rosses and Munros who then joined Thomas Mackenzie of Pluscardine (Seaforth's brother) when he descended on Inverness, expelled the parliament's garrison, and demolished the town walls. David Leslie was sent North to chase them back into Ross-shire, and he garrisoned Chanonry Castle and made terms with most of the rebels.

A year later, Montrose passed through Tain — as a defeated commander, prisoner of the parliamentary party. He had landed with an army in Caithness in mid-April, and Tain became the base for operations by Strachan and Halket who were ordered to oppose him. Five troops of horse assembled, and there was a council of war when Sutherland brought in 300 men and met Ross of Balnagown and Munro of Lemlair with another 400 between them. It was agreed that the earl should go back to Sutherland and protect his own country, while the horse with the clan levies should seek out the enemy.

On 27th April they marched west from Tain along the shore of the firth, and at Carbisdale, near the head of the Kyle of Sutherland, Montrose was surprised and defeated. He and a few companions managed to escape, and the victors returned with their other prisoners to Tain, where they were kept until Leslie arrived just in time to receive a message from Neil

MacLeod of Assynt that Montrose was his prisoner at Ardvreck, some 50 miles inland. General Holburn was sent to secure him, and on the 8th May — still wearing peasant's clothes, with a montero cap on his head and a ragged old dark reddish plaid round his shoulders — the soldier who had so often led the Highlanders to victory reached Tain. It is to be hoped that, if anyone in the town of the Rosses chose to jeer, some friendly eye would notice that when faced with insult Montrose 'never altered his countenance, but with a majesty and state beseeming him kept his countenance high'. He was lodged by Leslie for a night in Tain[1], and set out next day for Inverness and the long journey to the scaffold in Edinburgh.

Later that same year (1650), with a nation united against Cromwell under a king who was now himself a Covenanter, Parliament chose Pluscardine, Balnagown, the Master of Lovat and Lemlair as commanders of foot for the Inverness and Ross levies. Preparations were now made for the invasion of England on the king's behalf, and all the gentry in Scotland were summoned by Charles to his camp at Stirling. Balnagown raised the Rosses, and 'in doublets and breeches of striped redd hieland stuff with blew French bonnets on their heads' they joined the other clans in what became as near to being a national army as there had been for years. But it all ended in September at Worcester fight; Balnagown himself was taken, and for some time we hear less of the Rosses in the history of Tain. His death a couple of years later left a boy of nine to succeed to an estate burdened with debt.

Even before the news of the rout of the Scottish army reached the Highlands, Monck had almost completed the conquest of Scotland for Cromwell. Inverness was occupied about the end of November, and Dunnottar — the last place in Scotland which displayed the standard of Charles II— surrendered to Colonel Morgan in May 1652. The administration of the country was entrusted to eight commissioners, mostly military men, and representatives of both burgh and county met at Tain on 17th March to choose delegates to

---

1   Tradition says in a tall narrow house with crow-stepped gables which stood for nearly another 300 years, but was demolished in 1940 to make way for an air-raid shelter. It became known as 'The Ark', and stood at the corner of Hill Street and Morangie Road.

treat with them at Dalkeith for an incorporating union between Scotland and England. Tain's deputy David Ross, given full powers, accepted the 'tender' of union and promised that in the meantime the burgh would live peaceably under and give obedience to the authority of the Parliament of England as it was exercised in Scotland. The shire of Ross also assented, through its sheriff, Sir Robert Munro of Foulis, who had been appointed deputy.

Under the plan of union, which became effective later in the year, Scotland had thirty members only in the united Commonwealth Parliament, twenty for the shires and ten for the burghs. Tain shared a member with Dornoch, Dingwall, Inverness, Nairn, Elgin and Forres, and Ross with Sutherland and Cromarty; the burgh group 'elected' Robert Wolseley, commissary for Ayrshire, who was presumably one of Cromwell's 'friends' and was listed as being in favour of him accepting the royal title. The ordinance of union was not published in Edinburgh until May 1654, when the Protector was proclaimed, but by that time there had been another military diversion in the North.

General Middleton landed in Caithness in February with Charles II's commission to command his forces in Scotland. He had with him about sixty Scots officers, including experienced generals such as Sir George Monro and Dalyell, some ammunition, and a small supply of ready money. By mid-March Middleton had linked up at Dornoch with another royalist force under the Earl of Glencairn, and no doubt the people of Tain turned anxious eyes across the firth when a combined army of 3,500 foot and 1,500 horse was mustered and reviewed in such near proximity. They may even have witnessed a duel on horseback between Glencairn and Monro (who was a brother of Foulis), followed by another on the Dornoch links between two of their officers.

Morgan, who had been stationed with the garrison at Brahan, moved up to meet the enemy in what was described to the Protector as 'a wofull country', and advanced 'as farre as the Passe at Tayne' with his brigade; but he fell back on Dingwall in case Middleton's party might slip past him through the hills. By the time that Middleton eventually did march south, after returning to Caithness in search of recruits for the royal cause, Monck had come North and was operating in liaison with Morgan, and the fighting was ended by the surprise and defeat of Middleton at Lochgarry on 19th August.

On Morgan's return from Caithness, which he was ordered to make unserviceable as winter quarters for the royalists, his 'haill horse and foot' were quartered in the parishes of Tain and Edderton. It was harvest time, and there was complaint of 'cornes destroyed' and 'poor people plundered be the soggeris'. Morgan hit upon the expedient of making the nearby parishes which had not suffered — Fearn, Nigg and Tarbat — share in the losses, but they proved reluctant. An appeal was made to the convention, which also heard of Tain's low condition 'occasioned by fire and other exorbitant burdens sustained by them by Sir George Monro and his party'. The magistrates were accused, however, of neglecting to require people suspected of 'popisch recusancie' to abjure such principles and be fined.

In 1656, with some troops still quartered in Tain, the magistrates told Morgan (now commander-in-chief) that the 'poor towne is Ruined' and many have 'removit be reasone of their unabilitie to pay such heavy cesse and burdens of quartering'. At this juncture it must have seemed providential that a Dutch ship on her way to Spain should be wrecked and a great deal of her cargo scattered on 'our shoir and sands': but when the people of Tain tried to garner this unlooked-for harvest, backed by their magistrates claiming the ancient privilege of admiralty, an officious captain of horse interfered. The Dutch skipper and purser, hearing that the local kirk was ruinous and the town reduced to poverty, generously made over the shell of their ship, and the help of two Edinburgh lawyers was invoked 'to preserve our poor people from anie troubles'.

Exasperated beyond words, the magistrates told the convention that Tain was 'almost totallie dispeopled', and even asked that its name be deleted from the roll of burghs because of inability to maintain their liberties. The rule of the Commonwealth and Protectorate was a hard time for Tain, and it was probably with no great sorrow that they heard of Cromwell's death and the gradual disintegration of the government which he had founded.

Sir Thomas Urquhart of Cromarty is said to have died of a fit of laughter on hearing of the Restoration of Charles II, but there is no record or legend to tell us how Tain received the news. It meant an end to the exactions and disciplines of military dictatorship, indeed, but it was soon clear that the king meant to bring pressure to bear on the Scottish church. Bishops had been appointed before 1661 was out, the Covenants declared unlawful, and conventicles prohibited. Lay patronage, abolished in 1649, was restored, and all ministers admitted to parishes since then were required to obtain the recognition of both patrons and bishops.

Among about 270 ministers who refused to comply was Andrew Ross of Tain, and he was accordingly removed from his charge. Others in Ross-shire who declined to join what was called 'the king's church' were Thomas Ross of Kincardine, John MacKilligan of Fodderty, and Thomas Hog of Kiltearn — the last a man born in Tain 'of honest parents, native Highlanders, somewhat above the vulgar rank', who later made his name as a doughty Covenanter. More pliant clergy were soon found, but by 1665 there was a long list of defaulters — including Sir William Sinclair of Mey and his mother Lady Elizabeth — who had not paid their share of the cash needed for repairing the church of Tain and the kirkyard dyke, and who were going about openly in contempt of a Privy Council order declaring them rebels. The new Bishop of Ross, John Paterson from Aberdeen, felt the temper of the country about him to be 'very cloudy indeed'.

There were other signs that Ross-shire had not entirely settled down again under the monarchy. All the legislation adopted during the usurpation and the civil war, including the arrangements for making Ross a sheriffdom in 1649, had been annulled; but, while the old Act of 1504 was revived and the boundaries more exactly defined, future argument was invited by leaving blank the name of the burgh at which all

legal 'executions' or actions were to be made (although it was
laid down that courts were to be held at Dingwall, Tain or
Fortrose as the sheriff thought fit). There was some delay in
appointing a sheriff; the Earl of Moray, whose father had been
Sheriff of Inverness, seemed to think he had some claim to the
succession, for he entered Ross with a small force of gentry and
servants, and held courts at Tain and Dingwall. Glencairn, now
Chancellor, sternly ordered him to desist; and Charles, after
being reminded of the vacancy by the Privy Council, appointed
the Earl of Seaforth to be Sheriff-Principal of Ross. Apart from
this office, the Wardlaw minister commented, 'a farthing of the
King's mony he never saw, not so much as to repaire his
castle of Brahan, which the rebels spoild'.

Soon afterwards Seaforth came to Tain, attended by a
numerous party of Mackenzies and other supporters — with a
sprinkling of Munros, but not a single Ross — and the whole
company were received by the town council and admitted free
burgesses. Less than three years later, however, David Ross
of Balnagown and some of his clan charged Seaforth before the
Privy Council with various illegalities since his appointment,
complaining that the sheriff

> 'hes in prosecution of ane implacable malice, enter-
> tained by the name of M'Kenzie against the name of
> Rosse, essayed by acts of violence and injustice,
> shrouded under colour of his office and jurisdiction,
> and by frequent convocations under the pretence of
> assisting and executing his decreits, to provock and
> tempt the said compleaner and his name to ryse in
> armes, or to take such other course for their defence
> as might bring them under the compasse of the
> law: especially by a convocation made against the
> toune of Taine, the most part of the inhabitants being
> of the said compleaners name and relations.'

There is a clear indication of where this sheriff at least
would find it convenient to hold courts in Balnagown's
further complaint that his tenants in Strathcarron had had
to make the 25-mile journey to Dingwall in winter to answer

65

charges of poaching deer and fish, 'although the heid burgh of the shyre, viz. Taine, was the usuall place wherto the former Shreffes were in use to call the tenants of the said place' — and incidentally ten miles nearer to their homes.

But Seaforth, probably being warned to expect these grave accusations, promptly lodged such a powerful counter-complaint that the Privy Council at once ordered Balnagown to Edinburgh Castle as a prisoner. In May 1664, the sheriff told them, Balnagown and others mostly of his clan had gathered thirty or forty strong, and armed, at the moss of Milntoune (part of his Majesty's property) to destroy the peats won by Sir George Mackenzie's tenants; and on 30th May two or three hundred had gathered in and about Tain and 'continued in a bellicall and military posture' and would not lay down their arms nor disband until the sheriff went and 'dissipat' them in the king's name and authority. With Rosses and Mackenzies facing each other in 'bellicall' postures, the citizens may have sighed for the days of Morgan and Strachan.

In the summer of 1665 — with Balnagown safely lodged in prison — there 'comperit personallie' in the presence of provost and bailies the Right Reverend Father in God John Bishop of Ross, with his sub-dean and chancellor (both Mackenzies) and a few others; he was duly admitted a free burgess and guild brother as the sheriff had been. After what he termed the late 'State-quake', John Paterson had been quick to exhort the city fathers of Aberdeen in a Restoration sermon to pay the public 'assesses and impositions' with loyalty and cheerfulness ('What was paid to Usurpers', he said, 'let none grudge to pay to our just King'), and 'to sweep down many Spiders Webs, which the Iniquity of the late Times had woven'. Perhaps the magistrates of Tain proved themselves a less sympathetic audience.

Bishop Paterson (whose son was to be an archbishop) had a happy knack of printing his sermons — 'my warsh thoughts', as he called them — and dedicating them with humble genuflections to the great. Tain, while protesting its 'lowe conditione and povertie' to the Convention of Burghs, was perhaps also not above casting its bread on the waters by receiving sheriffs and bishops with flattering speeches (even if they looked with equal disfavour on both mitres and Mackenzies). They were now to deal with a notable scion of the house of Seaforth who was to have some influence in the town of the Rosses. In 1666 Sir George Mackenzie of Tarbat, who has already been mentioned, bought from Sinclair of Mey 'the superiority and feu farms of the town and kirklands of Taine pertaining to the heritable office of Bailiary thereof with the said office within the four girth crosses etc. within the immunity of the same'.

Sir George was to be no absentee, and within a month of signing the transfer, on his admission to an office which had 'remaned vacant thir divers yeires bygane', he was sitting with the provost and ordinary bailies in a burgh court at Tain and discharging the town 'of all bygane penalties and fynes and other dewtie dew to him'. A member of the Scots Parliament for Ross since 1661, Sir George was now out of favour because of Lauderdale's animosity (the Duke was once called *M'kenio mastix*, the scourge of the Mackenzies), but after many years of exclusion from office he rose to the chief management of Scots affairs and was created first Viscount Tarbat and then Earl of Cromartie.

Whether it was owing to influential friends at court or otherwise, the royal burgh of Tain received a new charter from Charles II dated 25th May 1671[1]. It quotes and confirms King James's charter of 1612, with its references to burgh lands, mussel scalps, and 'daill silver', and in addition grants to the provost, bailies etc. dues from lands held previously by the collegiate church of Tain (the James III charters of 1482 and 1487 are cited), and the common lands of Morrichmore, not specifically named in earlier deeds. Within a few years, by the unanimous wish of the inhabitants, the magistrates let these common lands for 2,000 merks and a yearly feu duty of £10 for the common good to Sir George Mackenzie and his heirs (they were defined as being bounded on three sides by water and on the fourth by the lands of Inverethie, Balcherry, Pitnellies, Balnagall and Newton); later, after a vexatious legal action and

1 This charter, sealed on 15th December 1672, is sometimes incorrectly dated 1675.

with the approval of the Convention of Burghs, they renounced any pretensions to the seaward part but reserved to themselves commonty rights in the landward part nearest to the burgh.

Soon afterwards the burgh became one of the first to have its arms recorded in the *Lyon Register* —'Gules, Saint Duthacus in long garments argent holding in his dexter hand a staff garnished with ivie in the sinister laid on his brest a book expanded proper.'

The period of repression which preceded the Revolution was known particularly in south-west Scotland as the 'Killing Time', but in Easter Ross too some conventicles or field preachings were held by the 'outed' ministers in spite of laws forbidding them. Hog and MacKilligan had their spells of imprisonment on the Bass Rock, and perhaps also Thomas Ross, who was later confined in the tolbooth of Tain although 'a sickly and tender person in hazard of his lyfe'. The magistrates were also ordered to imprison Sir John Munro of Foulis, an encourager of conventicles of such Falstaffian proportions that he earned the nick-name 'the Presbyterian mortar-piece' (the Privy Council simply called him 'a disorderly person not able to travel'); he may well have had the next cell to an embezzling collector of excise named John M'Leod, who was 'incarcerate within the tolbooth of Tayne to see if his imprisonment would induce him to restore the public money'.

An end to the religious struggle came with the landing of William of Orange at the end of 1688, and the flight of James. Presbyterian government was restored, and those who had been under a cloud emerged once more. Hog returned to his manse at Kiltearn, but Andrew Ross of Tain was not among the sixty 'outed' ministers who remained out of 350. The 'antediluvians', as they were banteringly called, held a general assembly in Edinburgh, and the business of reorganising the Church proceeded amicably.

Order was not restored throughout the country without an effort. A hurriedly summoned Convention of Estates gave David Ross of Balnagown a commission to be Sheriff of Ross 'till His Majesty's pleasure be known', and he and young Foulis were authorised to raise their kinsmen and followers.

When Claverhouse raised the standard for the exiled king, the Rosses helped to garrison Inverness, and Balnagown was made governor while General Hugh Mackay of Scourie went off in pursuit. Nearer home, with 500 men reported to be back at the old sport of cattle-lifting in Strathcarron, the whole countryside gathered to chase them away or give them battle: 'We are in such ane hurlie burlie heir', it was reported from Tain, 'that we doe not know what hand to turn us to'.

One of King William's first acts had been to ratify the privileges of the burghs and secure their rights to elect their own magistrates, and Tain was among the 65 burghs represented in his first Scots Parliament. With the 'glorious Revolution' the sun was once more shining on the Ross side of the hedge, and for a long period Balnagown and his friends had the chief influence in the affairs of the burgh.

7

The Tower

WITH changing forms of government, and the coming and going of armies, Tain men had gone far afield and their town had been seen by many strangers. The impressions of two outsiders have survived to give us a glimpse of the burgh in the middle of the seventeenth century, just before the fragmentary beginnings of the burgh records and a growing mass of local documents takes up the tale.

Richard Franck, one of Cromwell's soldiers, wrote in his curious *Northern Memoirs* of 'the town of Tayn in Ross, that equalizeth Dornoch for beautiful buildings, and as exemplary as any place for justice'. An angler and 'philanthropus', he wrote at length and with affectation, but his local information boils down to a statement that malefactors were drowned and not hanged (this was once the common form of execution for women in Scotland), that eggs were sold at 24 a penny, and that the soil of Ross had the quality of expelling rats. More exact, and less diffuse, was Thomas Tucker, who came to

Scotland to settle the excise and customs on the English model. He called Tain 'a small toune lyeing neere the mouth of a river of that name', and said that to it there came only 'it may bee a small barke once in a yeare from Leith, to fetch deales, which are brought down thither from the hills'.

That Tain's buildings should be favourably compared with those of the cathedral town across the firth is significant. The old collegiate church had safely survived the Reformation and the later campaign against 'monuments of idolatry', but by 1661 there was need of some 'reparatioune of church and steiple'. The chapel on the knoll beside the river and the smaller building in the kirkyard were probably already in ruins. One of the former church buildings in the vicinity may have been used as a grammar school, of which Partick Farquhar was master in 1646; there was also a 'musick school', and David Stewart who was appointed by the town council in 1673 to teach reading and writing, vocal music and arithmetic was still there to take the oath of allegiance to William III in 1693.

Dwelling houses, and even the tolbooth, were thatched with heather, and it was quite common for the most respectable citizens to have 'ane midding stead fornenst the door'. The 'King's high street' ran through the town, and some early control of building seems to have been exercised, as a merchant's 'uplifting of a stair from the high street to his house' in 1665 was thought to be prejudicial to the neighbours. At the heart of the town stood the market cross, of importance even before Tain became the head burgh of the shire, and now doubly so; here, in the presence of provost and magistrates, court officers cried 'three severall oyeses' to collect people to hear a proclamation, learn the time and place of a trial, or for other public intimations. A letter on pressing legal business took fourteen days between Tain and Edinburgh in 1696.

Dignity and informality were blended strangely in the town council. Each magistrate had a staff of office which was handed over on demitting office, and members were fined for absence — yet council meetings, even for the election of magistrates, might be held in the house of the provost or one of the bailies.

71

Burgesses were allowed to share in the trading privileges of the burgh, but the position might be inherited, for John Ross of Aldie was admitted in 1657 on producing his father's 'fredome'. Several different town clerks, each named Forrester, are on record in the first half of the century, and another official was the 'knockmaster' who looked after the town clock and bell.

It would be wrong to think that economic affairs were outside the ken of local government until recent times. In 1657 Tain was complaining against Dornoch for 'not useing diligence against unfree tredderis', and also against Wick and Thurso; in 1663 the council were banning the purchase of malt and 'aquavytie' in the landward parishes, as that would cause a loss to the burgh customs. By 1685, however, there were mutterings of revolt within the burgh itself against such exclusive claims, and it was reported that twenty 'unfree' traders 'keipes oppin chopes . . . and dayly trade . . . within and outwith the burgh to the great hurt and prejudice of the free men'. Later they even invaded the guildry loft in the parish church, and on Sunday sat there 'equaly with the persones that payed for making up the said loft'.

In one of its pleas of poverty to the Convention, Tain declared that 'within the tyme of the usurpation and his Majesties happy restoratione' the burgh was so 'depauperat and depopulat' that there were only three young men who professed any kind of trade whose stock usually exceeded £1,000 Scots in value, and that even they would be forced to give up. Yet lists for raising taxes dated 1659 and 1662 include a variety of trades—merchants, shoemakers, tailors, masons, weavers, maltmen, skinners, dyers and a host of others, including a snuff-maker, besides 34 owners and farmers of land—a total of nearly 100, which cannot be reckoned bad for a small burgh. Another reminder of the rural element is the 'Washing Burn', which ran through the middle of the burgh, and the sad tale of the ox in later years that was 'in the practice of eating clothes' and even swallowed a Hamburg gown.

But there may have been little room for smiles or finery in Tain at the time of the 'glorious Revolution'. Trade had been steadily declining, so that the burgh was only asked for half the share of Convention taxes that it had paid forty years before. It was a grey picture that a report for 1691 painted:—

'A great pairt of the building of this poor place is waist and turned ruinous, in soe far as many of the inhabitants and families were necessitat to quyt the towne by reasone of the stress of quartering of the forces and publict stress and impositiones . . . which occasioned the removeing of many from the place and extinguishing their families, and for want of payment of the said rest many more are lyck to be removed . . . the kirk steiple, councill and prison house of this burgh are so ruinous and demolished that they . . . cannot be made up in the same integrity it was formerlie without payment . . . which is a thing impossible . . . to doe without the christian and charitable supply of weel affected neighbours.'

As if all this were not enough, a series of natural disasters followed in quick succession. 'Ane great boat with the full loadening of merchant goods brought from Elgine' was lost at sea; cultivated land on the Morrich Mor was inundated by sand, no doubt mainly (as at Culbin and elsewhere) because bent, juniper and broom bushes were pulled up by the root for thatching; a bad harvest brought famine and misery, and Ross-shire families once well off were reduced to begging for their bread (fifteen commissioners of supply wrote in an excise report that 'every day multitudes were dyeing of meer hunger in the open feilds', grain had reached such a price 'as the like was never heard of in many ages and scarce since the world begane'); the town's tolbooth and steeple, being in a ruinous condition for several years, 'a pairt thereof did laitly fall in the night time whereby the prisoners therein were in great hazard of their lives and the fabric of the church much damnefied'; and finally 'a dreadful fire' in three or four hours destroyed the best part of the town. Here, if ever, was a burgh dogged by misfortune and in need of generous friends and powerful patrons.

George Viscount Tarbat, as heritable bailie of Tain, joined

with Provost Walter Ross in a petition to the Privy Council in 1703. Their steeple and tolbooth, they said, had had to be taken down, and they had started demolition in August but could not afford to rebuild without 'ane voluntar contribution' by all noblemen, gentlemen and others who might be pleased to assist. The upshot was that Tain was excused from the duty of accommodating prisoners for five years, and a collection to be taken in all the parish churches of the kingdom was authorised[1].

Such permission, soon backed up in this case by the Convention of Royal Burghs and the General Assembly of the Church, was not uncommon in those days to help in providing bridges, harbours, tolbooths and other public works. So one need see nothing sinister in the fact that two of the men who gave it were closely concerned with Easter Ross — Tarbat himself, and Lord Ross of Hawkhead, whose half-brother was the acknowledged heir to Balnagown. This 'old west country laird' had no traceable relationship with the clan chiefs (he belonged to a branch settled in Ayrshire since the fourteenth century), but he and his predecessors had long sought a connection with the Balnagown family, and secured large wadsets over their lands. Much to the disgust of indigenous Ross-shire gentry like Tarbat — who called him a hot-headed fool with 'his head turned round ever since he medled with Bellnagowan' — Lord Ross tried unsuccessfully to obtain a grant of the ancient earldom, which would have made him the feudal superior of his own chief and also of the Mackenzies and Munros; but he had better luck in his lesser ambition, to have him or his elected to Parliament for 'five shires and seven burghs in the north, and several others in the south'. Balnagown's

1 Rebuilding was about to begin when the fire occurred in 1706, and two years later the Convention of Burghs (who contributed 500 merks) were told that 'the said tolbuith and steeple with the pricket thereof consisting of six storry high, together with a counsell house of two houses hight adjoyned thereto, are finished to the securing of the plateforme and bartisane head of the said steeple'. Completion was delayed, Alexander Stronach the contractor having exceeded his estimate; stones were still being brought from the Hill of Tain in 1712, and it was not until 1733 that the bartizan was finally finished. The style is characteristically Scots with apparently Flemish influence (the resemblance to the more ornate Eschenheim tower at Frankfurt in Germany seems to be purely accidental), and the stone roofs studded with 'lucarnes' or imitation dormers are unusual. The steeple and the old church are Tain's two most distinguished buildings, and the former has been described as 'a sort of national monument' because it was made possible by a nation-wide appeal.

inherited influence was powerful, and it seems certain that Lord Ross put himself out to exploit it.

Before the Union of 1707, every royal burgh was entitled to return at least one 'commissioner' to the Scots Parliament. He was chosen by the town council, a purely self-perpetuating body whose provost and magistrates were by statute supposed to be 'honest and substantial burgesses, merchants and indwellers'. There are only five recorded attendances of a commissioner from Tain in the Parliaments before 1639 (the earliest, unnamed, in 1567); after that more regular appointments were made, and from the Restoration to the Union they continued regular throughout.

With the growing influence of Parliament after the Restoration, Scottish magnates began to covet the commissions that entitled them to take part in the deliberations in Edinburgh, which gave a man — and his family — a sense of importance among his fellows. Under the Act of Union, however, there were to be only fifteen burgh members for Scotland (one of the new groups comprised Tain, Dingwall, Dornoch, Wick and Kirkwall), and thirty for the shires: so the opportunities were more limited for men whose ambitions led them to seek public service or public prominence, and the market value of the seats rose accordingly.

A politician who could control three out of the five Northern Burghs was thus certain of a seat at Westminster. Each burgh appointed a delegate to attend an election meeting, but the election day itself was less important than the manoeuvrings for control of the councils which preceded it. Normally there were only two parliamentary candidates, and there were various ways of persuading the councils to select the 'right' man. If the numbers favouring each were known to be fairly even the issue might lie with one burgh only; and if so, something like municipal bribery — a new town clock seems to have been a popular line — or even a show of force was not out of order. Even the most predictable councils could not be neglected, lest an opponent work himself into their good graces.

It was not only the actual candidates for parliamentary honours themselves, but also anyone with a candidate to sponsor, who found it advisable to 'nurse' the councils. While there is little evidence of direct gifts being made to Tain or its councillors by the Balnagown family, there are several signs that they enjoyed, if they did not actually court, the gratitude of the people of the burgh. In April 1705, for instance, a town council deputation waited on David Ross of Balnagown to arrange the details of a concession offered them, whereby the town was to import goods from England in the ships that came to carry away the timber from the Balnagown woods as masts for her Majesty's ships; they expressed their thanks to and dependence on the laird, and said this was 'among the rest of your kyndnes showine to this toune'. Balnagown, who had succeeded fifty years before, was said by then to have been partly under the ministers' influence, and there is ample evidence that Lord Ross, even before the old laird's death, had won the goodwill of the presbytery by his 'support for the interest of the Gospel in their bounds'.

On the eve of the Union of the Parliaments, a sudden interest was shown by the local magnates in the composition of Tain town council. Up to Michaelmas 1706 its numbers had not exceeded fifteen, and in some years thirteen including provost, bailies, dean of guild and treasurer. But in that year Balnagown himself became provost, and the council was augmented to seventeen. In October 1707 six more councillors were added (they were William Lord Ross, William Lord Strathnaver, John Lord Macleod, along with two merchants and a wigmaker); next June — Balnagown still being provost — William Ross of Easterfearn, William Ross of Aldie, and Thomas Ross junior, merchant in Tain, were elected to 'officiate' in place of the deceased John Ross late provost, Bailie Alexander Ross 'being on death-bed', and the Hon. William Ross 'living at such a distance' that he could not attend the council: a total of twenty-six, including magistrates.

When this patrician council proceeded to appoint John Ross of Achnacloich to represent them at the Convention of Burghs, a rival council was set up and five or ten malcontents elected Bailie Æneas Macleod of Cadboll (local laird, lawyer, ex-M.P. and former town clerk of Edinburgh) as commissioner.

Cromartie had been highly displeased at the choice of Achnacloich, and it was really the old clan feud over again: 'the Mackenzies elected Cadboll for their representative, the party for the Rosses in that town sent Auchnacloich', Lord Fountainhall commented acidly when the matter came before the Court of Session.

The Convention of Burghs were clearly alive to the crisis which the new situation might give rise to in the election of magistrates and town councils. Finding that irregularities and abuses were causing trouble, they ordained in July 1708 that each royal burgh should send up its 'sett' or constitution for recording. Tain was obviously known to be one of the trouble spots, for two days earlier a committee had been appointed specifically to examine the position there so that a good understanding might be created in the burgh, and the citizens might 'live in amity and peace and within the due bounds and limits that is suitable to all the members of such incorporations'.

With the Provost of Inverness (Alexander Duff of Drummuir) as preses, and Tain's town clerk Charles Manson as clerk, the commissioners of Elgin, Forres, Dingwall and Fortrose duly met at Tain a month later. They called for the town books and records and inquired into Tain's election practice 'for forty years bypast', although they noted that the records were defective in several particulars. More serious, however, were the 'palpable encroachments' which had been made on the burgh's constitution since 1706, 'contrare to the setts of other well governed burghs' (Tain does not seem then to have had a written constitution of its own). They urged that the council should not in future exceed fifteen members, including the usual officers, and that 'they be all men qualified, conform to the acts and constitution of burrows, viz. that they be merchants, traffickers, actual residenters, tradesmen, inhabitants, or such persons as can gain or lose in the concerns of the burgh'. The provost, they recommended, should not hold office for more than three years, being chosen yearly by the council; bailies, dean of guild and treasurer not more than two years; and four of the old council should be turned off yearly at Michaelmas and replaced.

When the town council, with Balnagown as provost, met on 29th September, they adopted these suggestions as the new sett of the burgh of Tain, with one vital — and no doubt deliberate — exception. The phrase 'conform to the acts and constitutions of burghs' was followed by no explanatory and limiting definition, nor was this omission remarked on when the Convention ratified and approved the new sett, which was made (they recorded) 'conforme to the said burgh's antient constitution to the satisfaction of the inhabitants there'.

The new sett, so far as it went, was rigidly adhered to for more than eighty years, and as the Rosses were firmly in control they had no interest in changing it. When the five delegates met at Tain to elect a member to represent them in the first parliament of Great Britain, their choice fell on William Lord Strathnaver, son and heir of the Earl of Sutherland. His Tory opponent was Cromartie's younger son James (later Lord Royston), and mention by the old earl of a 'ryot committed by Ballnagown' suggests that there may have been some robust electioneering in Tain. Much in the election procedure was new, of course, as a result of the Union, and in 1709 Strathnaver was declared ineligible to sit in the Commons, being the eldest son of a peer; Hugh Rose of Kilravock, who had been elected for Ross-shire, was also unseated; and by 1710 the M.P. for the Northern Burghs was Colonel Robert Munro, younger of Foulis, and the M.P. for Ross-shire was General Charles Ross (Lord Ross's brother) who succeeded to Balnagown on the death of the old laird a year later. The Mackenzies' political star was waning, and with the sterner struggles of the ensuing years it was to set in blood.

When the last Stewart sovereign lay dying in London in the summer of 1714, her old servant — now simply the heritable bailie of Tain — was also near to death at his house of New Tarbat. They brought him news of the Queen's passing, and Cromartie shut himself up in his closet for three hours, was very melancholy when he came out, went to bed, and never rose again. The Elector of Hanover, whom Anne — much to the chagrin of the Jacobites — had named as her successor, was proclaimed as King George I in Tain on the 11th August, while all around men were mustering, arming, and setting guards about their homes. The old statesman, when they told him of this next day, wrote helplessly to his son:

'I profess I know not my duty as a shireff in the case, but waits either instruction or ordors from the superiors. . . Is it not lawful for heartie people to set up banefires when they please? Is it not lawful for a burgh to proclaim a king when they hear that he is declared to be a king? Is not hasty zeal on such occasiones meritorious?'

Little did the dying Cromartie or any of his neighbours in Tain think that a Stewart would be proclaimed at the same place almost within a year. Rumours of a Jacobite rising had been in the air for some time, and it soon became known that Mar had raised the standard of the exiled James on 6th September 1715. Tain's magistrates called on all able-bodied citizens between sixteen and sixty to muster in their best clothes and arms to receive orders, and they had the dean of guild seeking out all the powder and lead within the burgh. Seaforth called out the Mackenzies, and young Foulis assembled the loyal levies of his own and other clans at the bridge of Alness. Sutherland with about 300 men hastily collected, and Reay with another 300 of his own and more than 200 of General Ross's, had joined him; and on 29th September Tain sent '50 sufficient fencable men' with four days' rations under Captain Hugh Ross of Tollie to swell the Government forces, with more to follow.

This sounds a formidable array, and the total under Sutherland's command was reckoned at some 1,500. But Seaforth had collected double that number, having been joined by Sir Donald MacDonald of Sleat, The Chisholm, and Lord Duffus. After some parleying, a council of war was held at which Foulis and his friends were for fighting, but Sutherland thought the odds too heavy. While the earl marched off northwards with Reay, the Munros and the Rosses dispersed, and the way lay open for a Jacobite demonstration. Seaforth remained at hand in support, while Duffus marched into Tain with about four or five hundred Mackenzies, Chisholms and MacDonalds, and proclaimed the Pretender at the market cross. Two bailies — both Rosses, leaderless in the absence of the provost-general — held a hurried council meeting on 14th October, to consider a demand by Duffus for payment of £6 5s. 2d. Sterling (an odd sum) 'for his majestie King James VIII's use'; although judging themselves 'nowayes bound to honour that draught contrar to ther alledgiance to ther righteous sovraign King George', they yet resolved 'to prevent further trouble to the toune' by paying up.

James himself landed in Scotland in December, but the rising was all over by February. The uneasy interlude before the next one broke out may have seemed brief and uneventful by comparison, but what could have been more memorable, for example, than the events of 1721? It was then that a Tain bailie killed his namesake Hugh Ross of Achnacloich (they still point out the 'Duel Hill' on the Fendom road, where the footsteps used to be recut in the turf, even if some people mix up the combatants[1]); that another Bailie Ross (Easterfearn's brother, Robert) was captured in the hills near Kintail, and his nephew killed and others wounded, while trying to collect rents on one of the forfeited estates; and some Dingwall bailies were lodged in the tolbooth of Tain after an election scuffle which put any of Tain's efforts into the shade.

Such 'occupational risks' (as we might call them) may have been the reason why Tain was authorised in 1730 to elect a third bailie if they thought proper, as sometimes they were without a magistrate. A tightening-up of the byelaws and improvements to amenity are hinted at in the regulations regarding building on burgh land, repair and sale of ruinous houses, and collection of garbage, and in paving the ground 'before the town's shops' and 'thatching' the kirk with slates. A wave of infidelity which had reached the neighbourhood was traced to 'sundrie of the officers employed about His Majesty's revenues of customs and excise'; strong action was taken by the presbytery against the use of Sunday ferries for all but necessary journeys, and they saw heresy if not blasphemy in

1 William Ross of Shandwick was killed in a duel fought in London in 1790.

the burgh surgeon's habit of discussing metaphysics and theology in the argumentative way which he had heard great scholars and learned men use when he was at college. When he was ordered to appear in sackcloth before the congregation, however, his servant Rory Roy always came panting up to the church at the last moment with 'Lady Clyne has broken her leg', 'Donald Ross, Edderton, is bewitched or poisoned', or 'David Munro, Tarbat has fallen out of his booat and is drowned' — and away the surgeon must go to tend his patient, foiling the minister and kirk session for weeks if not for years.

Although poverty was still the excuse advanced to avoid further public burdens, there were signs of new trade in the burgh. In 1736 an expert weaver from Edinburgh was settled in Tain by the Trustees for Improving Fisheries and Manufactures, through the influence of the Master of Ross, with considerable materials and worklooms, to carry on the weaving of plain linen 'after the Dutch method' for at least four years, and every year to instruct a new journeyman weaver. In 1738 the Guildry Society was formed, to promote the dignity of trade as well as for the benefit of widows and children. The burgh mussel scalps were worth £90 in rent a year, and fishing boats came from as far off as Portknockie, Cullen, Portsoy, Whitehills and Banff; in 1739 the town council worked out a scheme of supervision by overseers, particularly to prevent strangers from damaging the beds by the use of shovels, and no doubt the 6d. per boat for attendance was well earned, and Bailie Malcolm deserved the new hat which the council gave him for his trouble in inspecting the scalps.

Politics showed much the same alignment, but with the forfeiture of Seaforth after the Fifteen and the bankruptcy of Cromartie in 1734 the Mackenzie influence was weaker and Macleod of Cadboll had assumed the mantle of Tain's tormentor. Sir Robert Munro of Foulis was unseated for the Northern Burghs in 1741, for although he had Tain and Kirkwall his opponent Charles Erskine of Tinwald had the other three. Erskine was unseated on petition (Dingwall had unwisely made Cromartie their delegate, but he was ineligible as a peer); the Government wanted a Lord Advocate in the Commons, and when Robert Craigie of Glendoick was chosen Sutherland wrote grandly asking him to stand for 'My Towns'. The by-election brought into the service of a Hanoverian king a law officer who was credited with Jacobite sympathies and did little to support the Government in the rebellion which broke out three years after he took office.

The Forty-five opened when Prince Charles landed in Eriskay on 23rd July, and about three weeks later the Lord President, Duncan Forbes, came north to his house of Culloden to rally resistance to the rebels. He needed commissions for the officers who would raise companies from the well-affected clans; they were eventually sent to him through Craigie as the senior member of the Government in Scotland, but this, and an eye-witness account of the battle of Prestonpans, was almost the only service performed by the M.P. for the Northern Burghs before hastening across the Border with the defeated General Cope, not to return until the rebellion had been crushed.

The Rosses were lukewarm and divided, and theirs was almost the last of the 'independent companies' to be completed. Neither Lord Ross nor his son the Master[1] (who was to command) was then in the North, so Forbes wrote to Inver-cassley (then provost of Tain) and William Baillie (factor for Balnagown). As soon as they had been advised that arms and money were available, about 100 Rosses were assembled, but young Malcolm Ross (whose father Pitcalnie[2] was nephew to Forbes and also heir-male of the Balnagown family) raised difficulties and eventually joined the Jacobites. The company dispersed, but Forbes then sent a letter for 'the gentlemen of the Name of Ross' by Munro of Culcairn (Sir Robert's brother), who met several of the clan at Tain and secured their promise to raise a company. The Master arrived in mid-December, but the

1   These were George 13th Lord Ross (1681-1754) and his son William (born c. 1720, suc. June and died Aug. 1754). The second son Charles had suc. his great-uncle Gen. Charles in Balnagown as a minor in 1732, and was killed at Fontenoy in June 1745 when only 24. His father, Lord Ross, had been 'Tutor of Balnagown' until Charles came of age, but probably never expected to be laird — hence perhaps some of the confusion over the independent company. The Balnagown estate remained with the Lockhart-Rosses, descended from the 13th Lord Ross's sister, until the death in 1942 of Sir Charles, inventor of the Ross rifle, who spent much of his life in Canada and the United States.

2   The Pitcalnie family's position was acknowledged by the grant of the chief arms of the name in 1903 to Miss Ethel Frances Sarah Williamson Ross of Pitcalnie (her sister and successor Miss Rosa Williamson Ross, now one of the oldest residents in Tain, was present at the first gathering of the clan in modern times, held at Tain in 1960).

company was not completed until 8th January, and he took part in its short and inglorious service from the 'Rout of Moy' to the surrender of Inverness on 20th February to the Jacobites, who had moved North after their last victory at Falkirk.

The Earl of Loudoun, commanding the Government forces in the North, just managed to slip out of Inverness as the Jacobites entered it. With the Lord President, Culcairn and some others he crossed by boat into the Black Isle under fire and made for Balnagown with such troops as remained with him. Sutherland had meantime come from Dunrobin to Tain, and he and the Tain people were asked to send all available boats to the Meikle Ferry for use as transports. On 23rd February Loudoun crossed over to Dornoch where his own regiment was quartered, while the President went to Overskibo; on the 26th 150 men were sent back to Tain 'who about noon made proclamation at the cross' and then returned.

Easter Ross was thus abandoned to the Jacobites, and there were said to have been 2,000 or 2,500 of them in the forces under Cromartie, later directed by the Duke of Perth, which spent 'some days' at Tain at the end of March. 'All the gentlemen of Ross shyre' were commanded to be there on the 27th to pay £5 sterling out of every £100 Scots of valuation, besides cess, crown rent and bishop rents; and the 'disorderly, wicked people (who consider us as enemies)' were successful in screwing about £60 sterling out of the burgh funds. The rebels seem to have scattered over the surrounding countryside, and Cadboll — who pleaded a convenient sickness — received a visit from 'the famous Mr M'Donald of Barisdale', who garrisoned his house and reduced his family papers to a disorder from which their owner thought them unlikely to recover.

All the local boats having been removed or destroyed, others were sent over from the Moray coast by the prince's orders. Led by Perth, and unobserved by the enemy owing to a thick fog, the rebels crossed into Sutherland on the last morning of March. The Government troops were taken completely by surprise, Sutherland got away by sea, Loudoun and the President by land, and some of Loudoun's regiment were taken prisoner. These successes were short-lived, but the damage they did and the consternation which they spread in the town of the Rosses left their mark. The Presbytery of Tain, when they met at the end of April for the first time for three months, held a special session 'for thanksgiving to the Lord for the signal and seasonable deliverance He was pleased to give unto these lands from Popery and slavery by the overthrow of the rebels at Culloden'.

Easter Ross settled down gradually to more peaceful times, although as late as 1751 a Ross clansman was arrested in a neighbouring parish and put in the tolbooth of Tain 'for wearing and using the Highland dress and arms' in defiance of the Act of Parliament. Cromartie was sentenced to death, but reprieved; Roderick MacCulloch of Glastullich, who had served under him as a captain, had a free pardon, but his estate was forfeited; young Malcolm Ross of Pitcalnie, who had been a colonel in the rebel army, was attainted. There were rewards of one kind or another for those who had remained well-affected: all heritable jurisdictions were abolished, and when claims to compensate for their loss were called for, Roderick Macleod of Cadboll distinguished himself by asking for a total of £12,000 — more than anyone else below the rank of earl, and £1,200 more than Sutherland's — of which £1,000 was for the bailiary of Tain which he had bought with the lands of Cromartie.

8

Cairn of Aulderg

IT is not unfitting that a chapter which will lead to the great era of parliamentary and burgh reform should begin with some account of an ancient ceremony that forms a unique link between the present and the past. The riding or perambulation of the marches was once a necessary safeguard and vindication of the right of property in land, and it has even been held to go back to the days when saintly relics were carried in procession round the boundaries of church lands marked at intervals by crosses where religious observances were held.

There is nothing left to tell whether Tain's perambulation of its bounds dates back to the days of sanctuary, or whether St. Duthac's bones were ever carried round its cross-marked perimeter. A yearly perambulation was stipulated in James VI's charter of 1588, and no doubt in the early days at least this was regularly carried out; within a year, in fact, there was a sharp reminder from the Convention that 'the provest, baillies, counsell, and communitie' of each burgh should once a

85

year 'perambulat thair haill marches, sua thatt they be nocht preugitt [prejudiced] by ony persoun thairin'.

As time went on, however, it seems to have been thought sufficient to make the perambulation periodic rather than annual; in the case of Tain it was, after all, a journey of some thirty miles, with ten or so halts for the transaction of burgh business. There are records of perambulations having been made and courts held on two days in successive years during the Protectorate (on 3rd and 8th July 1654, and 16th and 20th July 1655); there was a 'riding of the merches' in 1662, and perambulations in the following (and perhaps other) years:—1676, 1707, 1712, 1718, 1722, 1730, 1738, 1744, 1760, 1761, 1768, 1769, 1772 and 1797. It is not known when the custom was abandoned, but it must have been largely superseded by modern surveying methods.

Several days' notice of the date selected was given by tuck of drum through the town. Before the Forty-five all 'fencible' men were required to be ready with their best arms, under penalty of a fine of £10 Scots; there is a record of 1707 showing that more than eleven 'mutineers' had been fined for refusing to obey the orders of the officers or magistrates during a perambulation, although they had gathered under arms at one of the marches. Afterwards, as to carry arms was an offence, the procedure was — still by tuck of drum — to require all the inhabitants, heritors and feuars holding of the burgh to meet with the provost, magistrates, and council. In 1712 the meeting-place appointed was the Angel Hill, but in 1760 and 1797 it was the High Street or market cross, where suits were called and a court lawfully convened. Neighbouring gentlemen holding property of the burgh were informed, and on some occasions a heritor would join the party *en route*.

At one or more of the named points or 'court places' on the line of perambulation a formal burgh court was held — a form of open-air justice which seems to have become less common, if indeed it did not cease, after the '45. The town accounts for 1738 include a sum of £6 'by cash as instrument money taken in the clerk's hands at ten different court places when perambulating the town's marches'. The route taken would be well known, but it was the practice to follow the marches bounding the town's property 'as pointed out by the old inhabitants of the burgh and as contained in the town's charters from the Crown'. A specially keen watch was kept for any 'encroachments' — building houses on the town's commonty without licence, enclosing or fencing parts of it, sowing corn on the commonty, pasturing animals, or casting peat without permission, and so on. Formal protests would be made against such infringements of the burgh's rights, and where necessary the appropriate 'interruption' (as the lawyers called it) was carried out on the spot — stripping off part of a house already built, demolishing a dyke or house not completed or inhabited, pulling up a handful of corn, driving the animals away, or cutting and breaking up the peats. In more serious cases, a formal 'instrument of interruption' could be registered at Edinburgh as evidence that such a protest had been made.

The public accounts give some glimpses of the cost of each perambulation. The largest sum is £55 6s. for 'several necessaries furnished in the time of perambulating the town's marches' in 1738; a few years earlier 'expence at rideing the burgh's marches' was given at £21 14s. The burgh treasurer was more explicit in 1768 and 1769, when there are entries of 19s. 8d. for eighty bottles of porter and a bottle of whisky 'given to the people', and 'To the piper for playing before the magistrates and inhabitants at the perambulation 5s., and to Alex. Forbes for beating the drum 1s. 6d.'.

The actual words of the records, amplified here and there from maps of the marches in 1750, give the best idea of the route followed. Setting off from the Angel or Chapel Hill, they proceeded to Paul MacTyre's Hill, the first place where they held court, on or near the shore to the north or north-west of the Baads and west or north-west of Invereathie. From there they followed the shore to a hill called Poulnabodach, 'where the sea flows up a small stripe some chains'; round the north shore of the Morrich Mor to its south-east corner at Poulninich (otherwise Sheepford); and thence by Balnagall to St. Katherine's Cross, lying to the west side of the lands of

Lochslin or Loch Eye (the 1772 report omits St. Katherine's Cross and substitutes a 'black hillock lying to the south of Knockhellich'). Keeping on the north side of the loch, they then went to the cairn at the south-west corner of the Black Hill of (or above) Calrossie, and thence past the mosses of Glastullich and Pitmaduthy and along the high road to Torrannabuachil (or Knocknabochill), lying north-east of the moors of Logie; by 'the great high way' to Clasnacomerich (*clas na comraich*, hollow of the girth or sanctuary, also recorded as 'clash na caninarich'); and thereafter to Barnschlay (Bearns a' Chlaidhheimh, above Scotsburn and Lamington) and to Torvadroy, which seems to be the same as the cairn at the foot of Ulladill or Scotsburn glen.

At this point, about half-way round the marches, the 1768 report mentions 'dining in the usual place near Bealanalairg', and four years later it is more specifically called 'Knocknadiet', which appears in 1750 as 'Knock na dyte where the magistrates dine'. This must have been near the site of Culpleasant farm-house, perhaps on the wooded terrace overlooking the marshy hollow from which Tain now draws its water supply. In the centre of this hollow rises a knoll crowned with pine trees which may be the old 'court place' of Torvadroy, not far from the burn named in a 1610 charter 'Aldain-albainache or Scottismenisburne'. The old Tain burgh march seems to have run more to the west than the modern parish boundary over the ridge south of Culpleasant, perhaps by the large cairn of stones (Carnliath, the grey cairn, probably Dead Man's Cairn or Cairn na marrow of 1610) and then plunging down a fairly steep slope into Scotsburn glen.

Resuming the perambulation, detail of the rest of the route is less full in the old reports. From the dining place it wound up round Ben Garaig (or Garrick) and through the Lairgs of Tain to the valley of the Edderton burn; although the young Forestry Commission plantations grow thickly today, it is not hard to find Carn a' Chait, the next court place; thence they proceeded by the grounds of Rhanich round the north-west slopes of Edderton Hill, past a great march stone named 'Clachnabogane' in 1634, to the cairn of Aulderg, otherwise known as the Meikle Cairn or the cairn of Edderton, high on the hill above the Meikle Ferry. This was the 'ninth and last march', the 'last of the burgh quarter crosses', and from there the perambulation was completed by way of Cambuscurrie and Tarlogie to Tain, probably following the older road on the hillside.

One of the most persistent offenders against the burgh's property was the Laird of Cadboll, Æneas Macleod's son Roderick, who seems to have inherited some of his father's fancy for the law. In 1737 he had a charter of the lands and offices which he had acquired from the bankrupt Cromartie, and complaints were soon piling up against him and his tenants. The town council were particularly wroth in 1738 at finding 'a house built and encroaching upon the very girth cross [St. Katherine's] or boundary itself in high contempt of all law', and a summons against Cadboll was still pending when what he euphemistically called 'the commotions' intervened. He and the town were at it again in 1746, with a special court held at St. Katherine's Cross for the leading of evidence; and the protracted and expensive process before the courts came to be regarded by the Convention of Burghs as something of a crusade, for they put up twenty guineas and offered their own lawyer's help to allow Tain 'to vindicate its just rights' against Cadboll on account of the 'great oppression' met with from him.

By a judgment delivered in 1749 the Lords of Session, finding no proof of forty years' possession, ordained that the houses at St. Katherine's Cross were to be thrown down and the ground restored. Yet the 'manifest intrusions and encroachments made by Roderick Macleod of Cadboll and his tenants, mailers and servants' continued, and indeed they only seem to have ended with the death of this litigious laird in 1770.

The growing number of encroachments is a sign of an increasing interest in burgh property, and therefore a rise in its potential value, while the steps taken to prevent it — halting and ineffective as they sometimes were — show that the burgh realised that it was in danger of losing a marketable asset. A more business-like procedure was now taking the place of irregular council meetings, fines for non-attendance, spasmodic taxation, and unwilling collectors. Stent was more regularly imposed, and the burgh treasurer was given an extra salary to supervise its collection; there was an annual day for settling the burgh revenues — from the meal mill, mill lands, hill lands, customs, and the three shops under the town house — by public roup; and a small committee was appointed to settle all matters relating to the burgh.

There is good reason to connect these improvements with two men whose terms as provost covered most of the two decades from 1760 to 1780 — Admiral Sir John Lockhart Ross of Balnagown and David Ross of Invercassley, Lord Ankerville. As evidence of the Admiral's financial prowess, it is recorded that he told the Lords of the Admiralty, after engaging two French frigates each of greater gunpower than his single ship and driving them into Morlaix, that his officers had been better employed as seamen and fighting men than in book-keeping, and there had been no time for a minute attention to hourly expenditure of stores: their excusal from having accounts passed was said to be unique in the records of the Royal Navy. Ankerville's influence is less easy to assess, for, although he was for thirteen years a principal clerk of session and for nearly thirty years a judge, his contemporaries found him distinguished neither in his profession nor out of it, except for an unswerving devotion to the 'pleasures of the table'. Some of the credit may rather be due to members of the Baillie family, who were factors at Balnagown, for the council minutes show an even more striking improvement when Alexander Baillie of Knockbreck and General Sir Charles Ross of Balnagown alternated in the provostship between 1783 and 1813.

There were dangers as well as advantages, however, in the concentration of power in too few hands, and it was during the reign of these four provosts — to be more exact, from 1774 to 1816 — that a series of alienations of burgh property took place which were later severely criticised on the ground that, although the underlying motive may have been commendable, feus were made to members of the council by private bargain, and for inadequate prices. The record of one transaction, in which 17 acres were feued to the town clerk, David Ross, was even alleged to have been torn out of the burgh books, and no copy of it could be found when a Tain shoemaker, Alexander M'Eachan, later had to fight in the courts for the little possession of which he was subtenant.

As far back as 1713, the Convention had given the burgh authority to grant feus or long tacks of the moors belonging to them 'for the better improving thereof' (the Convention's right to do so has been questioned, as the lands concerned had been granted by the crown). At one time the burgh owned about 3,000 acres of moor ground in its neighbourhood; no rent was received, and the citizens exercised merely a right of pasturage, and of cutting 'feal and divot'. The heritors whose lands marched with the burgh's likewise claimed a right of commonty, and several of them were making considerable encroachments. In an attempt to bar such encroachments, to prevent prolonged lawsuits like that with Cadboll, and to create a permanent revenue, the town council resolved to offer those lands to be feued in the first place to neighbouring heritors, and in the next to the public. The feu duty was fixed at sixpence per acre, and in this way it appears that the greater part of the burgh lands were alienated.

A series of feus was granted in 1774, 1783, 1795, 1798, 1799 and 1800 to various magistrates and councillors, but the worst example came in the early years of the nineteenth century. William Murray, who served the burgh for more than forty years as councillor, treasurer, and latterly as provost, asked for a feu of a certain piece of ground while second bailie in 1805, offering slightly more than another offerer; at the very same meeting the town clerk presented the council with a charter ready made out for signature, and it was duly signed. In 1812 and 1817 the same magistrate was given two portions of the burgh market-place for his own private use, after he had explained that it would do no harm to lop off the portions on which he had set his eyes, as the space for the market had been found too large.

But the days of the self-perpetuating town councils were

nearing an end, and the writing was on the wall for those who could read it. A demand for burgh reform, which some people thought even more urgent than parliamentary reform, had been gaining ground since the early 1780s. It was frowned on by the Convention, and in Tain — a burgh which had in the past shown some of the Vicar of Bray's adaptability — there was strong resistance to any change. But some dissatisfaction was being shown at the way in which people other than merchants, who had no stake in the town, were being brought into the council. This came to a head in 1786, when three nominees put forward in the 'provost's list' by General Charles Ross — two were lairds, and the other lived in London — were negatived. Four years later a one-man revolt was pushed with even more vigour.

The objector was a man not easily ignored, as one might judge from the tall spare figure whose portrait looks down from the wall of the court where he reigned for sixty years. Donald Macleod of Geanies was called to the bar in 1768, married 'a lady of family' (Margaret Craufurd) in 1769, was elected to Tain town council in 1772, appointed Sheriff-Depute of the counties of Ross and Cromarty in 1774, and made convener of Ross in 1776. As representative in the male line of the Macleods of Assynt he was cousin to Roderick of Cadboll, but they were on such bad terms that when Cadboll made his tenants raise a great mound so that he could look down on his cousin's lands, Geanies replied by planting a belt of trees to block the view. In 1790, when the provost proposed to turn him and three others off in place of five nominees of his own, Geanies resolved to challenge the Balnagown interest on the town council.

A burgess and heritor himself, he objected in particular to the nomination of James Baillie, the Balnagown family lawyer in Edinburgh, and General Sir Hector Munro of Novar. In reply the magistrates pointed out that when the 1708 sett was approved there had been five country gentlemen on the council who had no residence in the burgh 'a qualification [they pointed out] neither required by the ancient charters, nor by the set then established, nor by the common law of the realm'. But their masterpiece of defence was surely the statement that:

> 'the office of counsellor in a little burgh is chiefly
> and almost entirely honorary, and it is much for the
> interest of the burgh that persons of character and
> distinction should be chosen.'

This frank admission, and the whole dispute, show plainly enough that other considerations besides the affairs of the burgh were involved in the choice of councillors.

Reference was made in the last chapter to the position of the individual burghs in the election of a parliamentary representative for the Northern Burghs. Tain in particular had an important place also in the choosing of a member for the shire, as such elections were made at the Michaelmas meeting of freeholders in the 'head burgh'. Although the name of the head burgh had been left blank in the Act of 1661 regarding the sheriffdom of Ross — courts were to be held at Dingwall, Tain and Fortrose at the sheriff's discretion — in practice these meetings were normally held at Tain. Between 1733 and 1828, for instance, 92 out of the 96 were held there, the only exceptions being in 1733 and 1755 (at Fortrose) and 1738 and 1753 (at Dingwall) — due either to some attempt at a system of rotation, or else with the object of transferring them to the burghs where the Mackenzies held sway and as far as possible from the centre of Ross interest.

Under the eighteenth century parliamentary system, a government was formed of ministers directly appointed by and solely responsible to the crown, and they had then to improvise a majority in the House of Commons. In the shires, just as with the burghs, political interests had to make their plans well in advance of an election year in order to carry the day; for it was only at the Michaelmas meetings that the roll of freeholders could be reviewed or amended, and only those whose names had been on it for at least a year were entitled to vote. It was common practice for one group to try to have the names of known opponents challenged and if possible removed, on the ground that they were not properly qualified, or to try to add the names of others favourable to their cause.

The blank in the Act made the shire of Ross peculiarly open to such manipulation. On a hint that there would be a move to change the place of meeting for the 1774 election, one side took the opinion of counsel, and the future Lords Braxfield and Covington (Robert Macqueen and Alexander Lockhart) gave it as their view that the place of meeting could not be changed by the freeholders themselves. Four years later Sir John Gordon of Invergordon proposed that the three burghs should submit their claims and pretensions for the opinion of counsel — Ilay Campbell and Andrew Crosbie were mentioned — but the freeholders seem to have done nothing officially.

The real row came in 1783, and produced a most undignified situation. Seaforth and Applecross, by a successful application to the commissioners of supply for dividing the valued rent of certain parts of their estates, had brought an 'inundation of made votes' from the Mackenzie country upon the roll. The 1782 Michaelmas meeting then proceeded to fix Dingwall as the place where the freeholders would meet next year, and the sheriff-clerk (a son of The Chisholm, and favourable to the Mackenzies) called it accordingly. Geanies, who as sheriff-depute found it convenient to have as much as possible of the county business transacted at Tain, objected and prevailed on seven freeholders — friends who lived in the same neighbourhood — to attend him at Tain. The result was that on 8th October one faction met under the sheriff at Tain, and the other met at Dingwall with the sheriff-clerk in attendance.

Not unnaturally, Geanies was furious at what he described as this 'public insult'. Along with Munro of Culcairn, whose name had been added to the roll by the Tain meeting, he raised an action against Chisholm in the Court of Session, and a decision of a sort was eventually obtained from the highest court in the land. Geanies said he had submitted a memorandum to the late Solicitor-General (Ilay Campbell), whose opinion was 'clear, distinct and decisive in favours of Tain'. Sheriff courts were usually held there, the sheriff-clerk for half a century back had resided there, and there the records were always kept. 'Dingwall', he argued, 'is at the foot of the mountains, which divide the cultivated from the barren and desert part of Ross-shire: and it is certain that for one gentleman's seat to the west of that line, there are ten to the east of it. And that the fact is that Tain is the more centrical to the inhabited part of Ross-shire, than Dingwall or Fortrose is'.

In reply, Chisholm pointed out that Dingwall had been the chief place and residence of the earls of Ross, and Fortrose of the bishops, while Tain had only a collegiate church. He quoted evidence that the head court had been in Dingwall in 1672-7 and 1680-2, 1688 and 1690, and the 1704 election was held there. Other public meetings, such as those of the commissioners of supply who laid on land tax and dealt with police matters and roads, went round the three burghs, proclamations were held at all three, and Ross was unique in that the sheriff's precept to hold parliamentary elections was executed at all three. A glance at the map was said to demolish Tain's geographical claim — 'the supposed desert to the west of Dingwall contains property far more valuable than the boasted tracts of cultivated ground to the eastward', and 'the neighbourhood of Dingwall is both better cultivated and better inhabited than the neighbourhood of Tain.'

These arguments, of which the echoes are often heard to this day, are now chiefly of academic interest. Early in 1784 the Lords of Session declared Tain to be the legal head burgh of the sheriffdom, and fined the sheriff-clerk £100 sterling for not having produced the minute-books at the meeting in Tain. Chisholm at once appealed to the House of Lords, who affirmed the lower court's interlocutor, but with a significant variation. While agreeing that the Tain meeting was the legal meeting of the freeholders, they ordered the words finding that Tain was the legal head burgh to be deleted. This was too fine a distinction for the town council, however, as is shown by the entry in the burgh accounts[1] of a tavern bill on 'the Lord Chancellor's affirming the decree of the Court of Session finding Tain the Head Burgh, £5 7s 8d'. It was to take another Act of Parliament to make the position clear beyond cavil.

The election of 1784, which had brought these matters to a head, is also of particular interest as having been the occasion

1 Macgill (no. 1273) dates this entry 1781, but the accounts for 1774-86 were all audited together, and apparently written up at one time.

of making a famous statesman the M.P. for the Northern Burghs. The rejection of Charles James Fox's East India Bill by the House of Lords, through the influence of George III, led to the resignation of the short-lived Fox-North coalition, and at the dissolution of parliament support for the Fox policy of limiting the influence of the crown was on the wane. As followers of Fox, Lord Ankerville and Sir Thomas Dundas (ancestor of the Zetland family) had joined forces to secure the votes of Tain, Dingwall and Kirkwall, while John Sinclair of Ulbster a devoted Pittite, controlled Dornoch and Wick in alliance with the Sutherland interest. The Foxites had intended to put up Ankerville's brother, Charles Ross of Morangie, for re-election — he had been M.P. since 1780 — but when the validity of their leader's election for Westminster on 17th April was questioned, Fox himself was hastily declared a candidate, enrolled as a burgess of Kirkwall, and elected at a meeting of delegates from the five burghs at Kirkwall on 26th April by three votes to two (Sinclair himself being the defeated candidate).

Fox declared that he only heard of Dundas's intention two days before he was chosen; and as he was determined to sit in that parliament, it would have been highly imprudent to trust only to Westminster once the famous 'scrutiny' had been set in train. This prolonged persecution — for such it virtually became (sparked off, incidentally, by a Westminster bailiff named Thomas Corbett, and continued with the approval of Pitt) — did not end until March 1786, and when a decision was given in his favour Fox at once resigned his seat for the Northern Burghs. His tenure of it was not one of the best periods of his parliamentary career, but the great orator spoke on a number of national issues as well as on the 'Westminster scrutiny', and in supporting the bill for restoring the estates forfeited after the Forty-five he described it as 'just, generous, politic, and humane', and suggested that its benefits should be made even wider.

This forgotten episode in the parliamentary history of the Highlands links Tain with the statesman who pressed the 'cause of the people' against the political power of the king. Fox regarded his unexpected election as 'owing to an accident' (no doubt a reference to his friendship with Sir Thomas Dundas), and shortly after learning the result he doubted whether to be 'chosen for Scotch boroughs' (as he called them) was a good thing or not; but all his friends thought it was, and their judgment seemed to him better than his own 'with respect to what regards *myself* in political matters'. What Tain thought of its most notable M.P. is not recorded: he may never have visited his northern constituency (although Dingwall made him a freeman within two months of his election); but he presented Tain with a portrait of himself, which disappeared some seventy years later on its way to Edinburgh for repair and renovation, and was never seen after reaching Invergordon by carrier's cart for shipment to Leith.

Sinclair, incidentally, had also been nominated for two constituencies, and although he had already been returned for the 'pocket borough' of Lostwithiel he tried to have Fox unseated for the Northern Burghs. He complained that Fox's burgess ticket, though dated 23rd April, was not confirmed by the town council until two days after the election, and that the Kirkwall delegate was irregularly appointed; but he withdrew additional objections (which were unsupported by any evidence) that the Tain and Dingwall votes were also incompetent, and that Fox's success was due to 'corrupt agreements and other illegal practices on the part of his friends which amounted to bribery'. Sinclair did not secure election for himself, however, and in the by-election which followed Fox's resignation a Sinclair-Sutherland nominee was defeated by George Ross of Cromarty. Party alignments were now taking the place of family attachments, and when this remarkable man died within three months of his election, the young heir of Balnagown, Charles Lockhart Ross, won the seat for the Pitt administration by defeating his Fox-North namesake of Morangie. He was followed from 1796-1802 by William Dundas (later M.P. for Edinburgh and Lord Clerk Register of Scotland, three times provost of Tain between 1814 and 1829), whose uncle Henry Dundas, Viscount Melville, was Pitt's able 'manager' for Scotland.

Without recounting the story of later elections, or even naming all those who sat for the Northern Burghs, it may be noted that the revival of the old head burgh controversy may have made Tain realise the awkwardness of sharing an M.P. with her rival. A new jail and courthouse had been built next to the old one in 1825-26, but public indignation at prison conditions in Scotland generally led to a Bill being introduced into parliament by the Lord Advocate (Sir William Rae) to provide at least one sufficient jail in each county. Its location was to be left to the commissioners of supply and justices of the peace to decide, and Tain took alarm on learning that the convener of Ross, Colin Mackenzie of Kilcoy, had told the Lord Advocate that there was no head burgh of the county, and that Dingwall was 'the most centrical' location.

The papers relating to the 1784 case were exhumed, and the town clerk, Alexander Taylor, was instructed to draw up a memorial stating Tain's claim to be head burgh of Ross and the best place for the county jail, in reply to arguments put forward for Dingwall by the gentlemen of Wester Ross. The document, approved on 12th March, 1829, was a powerful piece of special pleading, ranging over the whole field of law, history, geography and even etymology: it quoted the inquest of 1439, 'lately discovered'; it pointed out that Tain was named first in the rolls of the Scottish Parliament, and was 'one of the three Burghs which refused to accede to the project of selling their King'; the record of freeholders' meetings since 1733 was recited; it declared that Tain was found to be head burgh 'by a solemn and unanimous decision of the Supreme Court', and that the House of Lords had affirmed on appeal that it was the legal place of meeting for the freeholders; and even the old tongue was invoked with the bold pronouncement that 'the very name of Tain in the Gaelic and ancient language of the country is Ball'n'Dhuich, which literally signifies "The County Town". In reply to the argument that Tain was in the eastern extremity of an extensive county, it pointed out that there were sixteen miles of well-cultivated and populous country to the east of it, and even Lochbroom on the west coast 'is nearer to Tain by a good road than it is to Dingwall by a bad road'; and that the nine parishes in the presbytery of Tain paid a yearly rent to the landlords of upwards of £30,000.

James Loch, who began a spell of 22 years as M.P. for the Northern Burghs in 1830, confessed himself as 'greatly embarrassed' on finding the contending claims of Tain and Dingwall so diametrically opposed to each other, and decided that neutrality was his safest course. Loch was commissioner on the vast estates of the Marchioness of Stafford (already Countess and later also Duchess of Sutherland), and managed his five constituent burghs so well that they kept him in parliament for twenty-two years. Tain town council's minute shows that he offered himself for their suffrages as follows:—

'My pretensions are a connection of 17 years standing with the North of Scotland, commenced through the friendship of the Marquess of Stafford, and having during that period had a considerable share in forwarding many of the public improvements connected with the district generally, as well as with the county of Sutherland in particular, to promote the interests of which was my principal duty and concern.'

Enough was already known about Loch's methods in carrying out the 'Sutherland clearances' to show that those who chose him as their representative at Westminster were unlikely to be enthusiasts for reform. He was hardly in his seat when the storm burst, and Tain town council among others was being asked to hold meetings for the purpose of expressing approval of the plans brought forward by the Grey administration. Such applications were twice refused at the beginning of 1831, although 'moderate and constitutional' reform was not ruled out. When a petition for reform was circulated through the town and attracted 200 signatures, the council informed Loch that not more than twenty held £100 worth of property, and added that the great majority of those signing were schoolboys, apprentices, and 'people who from their rank and education are entirely incapable of forming any opinion whatever upon the subject of the petition'.

But the Canutes of Tain could not stem the tide. Lord Grey's government, pledged to peace, retrenchment and reform, produced the first Bill in March 1831; its defeat led to a dissolution and the return of a parliament still more devoted to reform. It was Tain's turn to be the returning burgh for the group (as it had been in 1707), as well as the legal place of meeting for the freeholders to elect a member for the shire. Loch was returned for the burghs; and Seaforth, elected for Ross as an avowed champion of reform, was carried in triumph when the result was declared on 25th May.

It was the last parliamentary election under the old system, for after various vicissitudes the Reform Bill passed the House of Lords in June 1832, and the Scottish measure, following the same lines, passed on 17th July. The narrow county franchise and the town councils' right of election disappeared, and the vote in the burghs went to householders with £10 worth of property. Cromarty, as one of a new class of non-royal or 'parliamentary' burghs, joined the group to which Tain belonged.

Loch and Seaforth were duly re-elected for the burghs and the county, and with a Liberal administration supported by 43 Scottish M.P.s out of 53 the business of burgh reform was soon tackled. It was logical that self-election, discarded in the choosing of M.P.s, should be abandoned as the basis of municipal government. The existence of nearly standard burgh 'setts' or constitutions made the task easier in Scotland than in England, and in 1833 the right of electing the town councils was conferred on £10 householders, one-third of the councillors were to retire each year, and the first elections under the new system were appointed to take place in November.

9

Tain Royal Academy

IN spite of stirrings within its borders, administrative reform had to be imposed on Tain from without. But in a number of ways the burgh had been progressing, and the period reviewed in the last chapter also saw the old church replaced by a new, the birth of Tain Royal Academy, the development of trade and commerce, and local craftsmen flourishing whose work is still admired today.

The collegiate church had undergone many changes since it was built away back in the fourteenth century, and it would hardly seem the same place either to those who had carried out the Roman ritual within its walls, or to the more recent episcopal incumbents. The last of these had been deposed in 1699, and Hugh Munro, the minister of Tarbat, was called to Tain, much against the wishes of his own congregation. In the end he had to be forcibly translated in 1701, being (according to a persistent tradition) actually taken out of his old pulpit, carried in triumph to Tain, and placed in the

Regent Moray's pulpit to preach the sermon he was to have delivered at Tarbat.

By 1706 there were enough presbyterian ministers — four out of the eight parishes being filled — for the district of Easter Ross to be erected into the presbytery of Tain. All but a few of the common people were quite illiterate, and spoke nothing but Gaelic, but their minister was able to report a 'legal school' in Tain when the newly-erected Synod of Ross and Sutherland inquired in 1707 how far the Act for erecting and endowing a school in every parish had been implemented. An attractive feature of Hugh Munro's ministry is the way in which his flock supported a variety of good causes beyond their bounds, aiding the sufferers by a fire in the Canongate of Edinburgh, an Inverness shipmaster and his crew who were slaves in a galley, new churches to be built in north-west Sutherland, and the Scots congregation in New York.

The fabric of the church—especially the interior — had also changed beyond all recognition by the eighteenth century. Round the old pulpit, on a floor area 71 feet long from east to west and 23 feet 9 inches wide, there were ranged the seats (already possessed 'time out of mind') of the chief burghers, guildry and trades in the south half, and in the north those allotted to the heritors of the landward part of the parish and their families. Above at the west end the 'commons' loft'—for the tenants and servants of both heritors and burghers — occupied the full width of the church, and, although the walls were by no means filled, there were also the provost's loft and one for the skinners of the town.

When the old church needed repair, it was the custom for the burgh to pay one half of the cost and the landward heritors the other. Repairs were needed in 1754, and a report prepared by 'John Robert and James Adams, architects, Fort George' (the most famous brothers in the history of Scots architecture, then busy with one of their chief Government commissions in the North) gives some idea of the state of the church. Although supported by buttresses, the side wall next to the 'steep bank or precipice' was reported as hanging nine inches over its base, despite the fact that the two angles seemed perpendicular. In the circular window at the east end the uppermost arch stone had dropped and caused a crack, and they feared that a 'push' of the timber roof had occurred owing to the weight of the thick slate covering. The Adam brothers' advice was that the overhanging wall should be straightened, and the heavy slates replaced with lighter and more durable ones from Easdale in Argyll; this was probably done, as stent was raised for a new roof in 1755.

This was a difficult time for the minister, John Sutherland, who had come to Tain in 1752 after a fruitful ministry in Golspie. Patronage had been restored by Act of Parliament in 1712, but few patrons in the North exercised it; a presentation by George II to the parish of Nigg, however, led to a four-year dispute which ended with the presbytery being rebuked by the General Assembly and ordered to admit the 'intruded' minister against the wishes of his congregation. As moderator of presbytery, Sutherland had to preside at the unpopular induction, and it is said that feeling was so strong that most of Sutherland's own people boycotted his ministry in Tain for three months thereafter. He had started badly by earning a personal rebuke from the presbytery for breach of promise of marriage (with a daughter of Captain Daniel Macleod of Geanies); another episode of his ministry, although unedifying in itself, is useful as showing how strong was the demand for seats in the church in those days.

As early as 1730 the trouble-making Cadboll had complained of want of room. He maintained that his valuation as chief heritor in the parish entitled him to 32 feet of the landward share of the area below, and as much above for lofts, whereas he only had about 12 feet below and 'not one inch' above for himself and upwards of 105 families of tenants. When he was offered space for a loft, he said, Ross of Aldie threatened criminal prosecution if he even touched the 'high cornice of the corner of his seat' immediately below; then, when the kirk session agreed to give him pretty nearly what he asked for, the town council objected. He took them to the Court of Session with such success that he not only got room in the area and above it, but was allowed to deface the ancient shrine by 'hewing out' an entry door in the window on the north wall and building an outside stair leading to it.

All that the kirk session drew the line at was adding a second tier of galleries, 'as the condition of the fabrick will not admit of any *loft above lofts*'. But even this safeguard was set aside before the old church was abandoned. From 1797 Tain had one of its most famous ministers, Angus MacIntosh, once a student in Balnagown and then minister of a Gaelic chapel in Glasgow, who exercised a wide and deep influence in the town and beyond it. The Good Regent's pulpit knew his tall and massive figure, dark expressive face, and solemn and dignified bearing for many years, but the man who had preached in the largest churches in Scotland found it a greater strain to preach in his own cramped, draughty, ill-lit church, crowded (as he wrote) 'even with galleries above galleries'. In a petition to the presbytery he pointed out that a church which could accommodate only 720 persons was far too small for a population which had risen to 2,333 in the town and parish by 1810.

James Smith, an Inverness architect, was ready to extend the old church to accommodate about 900 people, but he recommended the magistrates and heritors to build anew on a different site. They fixed on a piece of ground at the east end of the burgh, where the neatly-planned 'New Town' had been impinging for more than a decade on green fields belonging to Donald Macleod of Geanies, who no doubt profited handsomely. There, to James Smith's plans, a Peterhead firm of contractors named Mitchell built the new church, which was completed in 1814 and served the parish for the next 130 years. An unecclesastical looking building, with square corner towers and no spire, it was perhaps more suited to its modern use as a town hall; but at least it ended the uncomfortable crowding of its predecessor.

Meanwhile there was progress too in education, which gave the town a building of which it had every reason to be proud, also designed by James Smith. Tain already had its own grammar and English schools, and towards the end of the eighteenth century there was also a schoolmistress or 'sub-doctrix'. But the schoolhouse was reported to be 'ruinous for want of thatch' in 1776, and in 1791 it was not only far too small, but the scholars had no place to 'divert' themselves but the churchyard, where they were apt to break the church windows and hurt themselves by jumping over the gravestones.

It must have been about the turn of the century that the idea of establishing an academy at Tain took shape in the minds of a number of gentlemen of the county of Ross. A liberal education was regarded as a stimulus to the sciences, arts, agriculture and manufacturers of the country, and indeed of Britain's expanding empire overseas, as well as for its own sake and for the benefits it conferred on the individual. In this enterprise a Mackenzie chief was at last on Tain's side, for the aspirations of the founders were eloquently expressed by Seaforth himself (a British peer and a general in the army):—

'... Those gentlemen had a just reliance on the beneficence and good sense of the opulent natives of the Highlands; they knew both their hearts and heads would be deeply interested when such a project was laid before them; for that heart must have little of the patriotic Highland glow that does not warm at the idea of lifting so many of their youthful neighbours out of ignorance and inutility into knowledge and importance, and the head must be weak that cannot see the great good that would result from keeping such a circulation of money in the country, and the still greater future good that would result from the success in life that might be expected to attend many of those youths the Academy would send into the world ...'

But the real founder of the academy was Hugh Rose of Glastullich (later Hugh Ross of Cromarty), who lived at Calrossie and played a notable part in the life of Tain. His father, who died when Hugh was only seven, had been parish minister from 1770 to 1774, and his mother was a daughter of David MacCulloch of Glastullich. As a young man, Hugh went out to the West Indies, where he had some official post connected with the British forces, and made 'a fortune with which he was satisfied' in the course of a very short period with a company of which he was admitted a partner. Returning home for the recovery of his health, he purchased the estates of Calrossie, Glastullich, Arabella (called after his wife), Tarlogie, Morangie and others; his 'improvements' vied with those on Balnagown, and Sir John Sinclair's daughter saw so many ploughs going in one field that the effect was like a ploughing match, although 'his farming establishment is now reduced to only forty pairs of horses'. Hugh Rose is said to have acquired a fortune by his first wife (who 'in the act of preparing medicine for the relief of a sick and indigent family suddenly expired', according to the epitaph on her monument in the old church); and by his second marriage — to Miss Munro of Culcairn — he succeeded to the Cromarty estates. He was another of these Ross-shire lairds who loved a lawsuit; the pleadings and documents relating to a dispute which arose out of a partnership in the West Indies with a son of Geanies filled a printed volume two inches thick, and a bound copy of their correspondence lay on the drawing-room table at Geanies for the entertainment of every visitor to the house.

But the future foes were close collaborators over the inception of Tain academy. Glastullich in particular, along with his family and friends, contributed handsomely to its foundation, and collected large subscriptions from all quarters of the globe. Very soon a sum was subscribed which, with subsequent accumulation, amounted to above £7,000. The county assessed itself in £1,000, and the burgh gave 100 guineas and settled £25 a year on the rising institution. In the first year's subscription list, for 1800, while Seaforth and Balnagown contributed £50 each, it was noticed that Donald Macleod of Geanies put up £105, and Hugh Rose of Glastullich £210.

Even the siting of the academy was left to private generosity, although the town was prepared to provide a piece of ground in Little Tain. But Lord Ankerville gave the promoters a fine park 'leading to the shore by MacMeaklan's Well', and it was decided that the building should be erected there. Smith's plans were approved in April 1808, when funds stood at nearly £8,000, and a crown charter was granted — following the precedent of Inverness Royal Academy — in the name of George III on 6th April, 1809.

The foundation stone was laid on 18th July, 1810 by Alexander Baillie, late provost, and the academy was opened with about 130 pupils on 18th February 1813. The building was spacious and elegant, the centre part built and fitted up with classrooms 13 feet high and 28 feet wide; there were an examination hall and rector's rooms on a modest scale, and 'philosophical and geographical apparatus' for the cultivation of the higher branches of science. A small observatory dome seen in the early pictures of the academy was removed in 1826, as it was found to be pressing down on the roof and had proved 'completely useless' for its intended purpose.

For the selection of a suitable rector and three experienced teachers, a special examination was held before Principal Baird and two of the professors of Edinburgh University. Teaching was then a common preliminary to the ministry, and the first two rectors — whose salary was then £90 per annum plus £20 in lieu of house and garden — only lasted four years each: Alexander Macpherson, a farmer's son from Gairloch and a graduate of King's College, Aberdeen, who was called to Golspie parish, and Alexander Cameron from Aberdeen, who became minister of Edderton. Undeterred by this leakage, the directors chose another student of divinity, William Ritchie, who was rector from 1821 to 1831, and showed an experimental bent which even went the length of providing a substitute to perform his duties while he attended scientific lectures in Paris. He persuaded the directors to acquire apparatus for exploring the properties of fluids, and to 'illustrate the fascinating subjects of electricity and galvanism and the principles of chemistry' (which had been taught with success at Perth Academy); and he gave public lectures for the enlightenment of 'the respectable inhabitants of Tain', to which mechanics were admitted free on promising to make small models of machines for use in the academy, while those who paid fees helped to meet the cost of enclosing the academy park. Ritchie's abilities earned him an early fellowship of the Royal Society, and the directors cannot have been greatly surprised when he accepted the post of Professor of Natural and Experimental Philosophy in London; as his successor they appointed John Noble, Rhinie, who had been interim rector in 1826, only to lose him to the parish of Fodderty two years later.

Apart from the rector, the original staff held together for nearly twenty years. Alexander Beattie, who had been teacher of the English school at Tain, became the burgh's unofficial poet laureate[1], and resigned in 1831; John Mackinlay, from Kirkintilloch, who taught writing and arithmetic, followed for health reasons three years later; while Adam Gibson, who had come from Forfar grammar school and took the Greek and Latin classes, dabbled in politics and narrowly escaped dismissal in 1819 for taking too active a part in an 'absurd institution' called the 'Transatlantic Association'; he successfully challenged another attempt to get rid of him for intemperance in 1835, and was finally dismissed in 1837. Gibson claimed that the academy was a public school in which the teachers held office for life, and the directors were forced to spend about £1,000 in defending their decision in both the Court of Session and the House of Lords, which found in their favour in March 1840.

A further appeal for support, made in 1816, when the academy had above 240 scholars from all over the North of Scotland, was directed mainly towards building up a library on foundations laid by private donors. In approaching the public again twelve years later there was a special word for 'patriotic young gentlemen' who were now beginning to reap the fruits of their education at the academy: 'Should her earnest appeal reach the distant Isles of the Atlantic or the Banks of the Ganges or Indus, and there meet one "faithful and true" son of the North, it will not have been sent in vain.'

One of the remarkable things about Tain Royal Academy is the support which it received in its infancy, and indeed still enjoys today, from friends and former pupils at the ends of the earth. Thirteen holders of property in the United States or the

---

1 Of his published verses, one celebrating the beneficence of John Ross, a native of Tain in London who sent £100 annually for the poor of the parish, includes the lines —

> 'Where Tain's cinque spires in antique grandeur rise,
> And point their conic columns to the skies,
> As land-marks to the veering barks, that glide
> Through syrtes (quicksands) of the Gizzen Briggs to guide'.

West Indies, all connected with the North of Scotland, had been among the original subscribers of £50 and upwards. Lord Seaforth was Governor of Barbados from 1800 to 1806, and may well have used his influence among West Indian merchants there and in London, while Glastullich and Geanies were deeply involved in cotton, coffee and sugar plantations — named after their estates at home — in what is now the independent state of Guyana. A list of subscribers from Berbice, including the West Coast and Demerara, forwarded in 1814, showed that nearly £1,000 was to come from Scots in that colony, where the subscribers' plantations bore such names as Alness, Creich, Dunrobin, Foulis, Golspie, Kilmorack and Novar. Tain itself had been transplanted to the tropics, for the papers in the Geanies-Glastullich litigation mention a plantation of that name.

The war with France, merging into the long struggle with Napoleon, was widening the horizons of many a home-dwelling Scot, sending them to swell the ranks of the army and navy or to seek their fortunes in the expanding territories overseas. At the same time volunteers were enrolled for home defence, militia balloted for, and the recruiting officers were busy (a fracas in 1776, when Lieut.-Colonel Alexander Ross of Calrossie found himself in the tolbooth on a charge of murdering one of the town guard, was long remembered although he was acquitted). Prices rose steadily, and owing to the blockade the price of oatmeal in Ross-shire doubled between 1799 and 1809. Foreign commodities, such as could be got, came through Inverness for most of the Highland area, but Tain continued to be a busy centre for home produce, even if the shop tax returns for 1785/6 and 1786/7 only show two shops in the burgh (owned by Benjamin Ross and George Murray).

The banks began to establish branches at Tain in the 1790s, and Hugh Miller recalled how in later years the young bank clerks from Tain and Cromarty used to meet at midnight on the hill of Scotsburn to square the week's issue of notes. One at least of the pair carried a loaded pistol in his pocket; but by the turn of the century the significant phrase 'The law has come to Tain' was already well-established, indicating that the old days 'when they should take who have the power, and they should keep who can' were over. Patrick Thomson and John Black, 'writers in Tain', showed that the city lawyers did not have a monopoly of legal lore by producing in 1806 a little treatise on 'the office of a sheriff-officer, and also of a commissary, town, dean of guild, and baron officer', which they dedicated to Geanies as sheriff-depute.

Tain was also making a name for itself as one of the provincial centres where competent local craftsmen were at work, their products including elegant clocks and silverware. Hugh Ross, who was a man of property by 1751, used as his mark part of the burgh seal (half the figure of St. Duthac); he must have had an extensive business, for at a roup of 1787 after his death the stock included rings, table spoons, tongs, candlesticks, buckles, a silver-mounted snuff box and 47 'silver hearts' of a type used as engagement gifts; some at least of these were probably his own work, and he is known to have made quaichs and teapots. Other Tain silversmiths included Alexander Stewart and R. M. Wilkie, but the craft decayed after a statute of 1836 required all plate made in Scotland to be hall-marked in either Edinburgh or Glasgow. Collections of Tain silver are much prized today; and there is a dirk with silver mounting of Tain origin in the collection of Her Majesty the Queen.

Another Tain craftsman was John Ross, watch and clock maker, whose clocks from the later part of the eighteenth century are prized by collectors, and who had earlier offered to finish a musical eight-day clock 'that will play such twelve tunes as Geanies shall appoint'. It was a sign of more prosperous times in Tain that the town could offer a living for such men, as well as for the humbler and more necessary tradesmen ('a very useful member of the community', wrote a pawky presbytery clerk of a tailor who was an elder, session clerk and precentor — 'especially in so cold a climate as that in which we live').

Another important event was the establishment of the St. Duthus Lodge of Freemasons (No. 82), whose charter of erection, dated 2nd February 1761, was signed at St. Mary's in Edinburgh by the Grand Master Mason, David Earl of Leven. All the expenses of obtaining the charter and presenting a set of clothing and jewels 'of the genteelest kind' were paid by the future Lord Ankerville, who was the first master, with Hugh MacFarquhar (surgeon in Tain from 1744 to 1794) as his deputy. David Ross, merchant in Philadelphia, was 'passed fellow-craft' in 1762, and twenty years later Captain Johan Frederick Iben of Stralsund, in Swedish Pomerania, gave £3 to purchase a chair for the master to be placed in the lodge when built. The Guildry of Tain had offered to lend money for this purpose in 1781, and the 'Knight's House' (on the site of the south part of the modern Royal Hotel) was rebuilt as a masonic lodge, the foundation stone being laid in 1783.

A healthy awareness of outside opinion was growing in the burgh. A piece of waste ground near the steeple 'so situate as to be in view of all strangers and travelers' was described in 1777 as 'an eyesore'. As the market cross encroached on the street and prevented wheel carriages from passing, it was resolved in 1778 to take it down and to fix 'the long stone and lion' on a pedestal on the summit of the same spot, while the surrounding walls were removed. Visitors were beginning to come, too, such as the Irish Bishop Pococke, who thought Tain a poor town in 1760, though pleasantly situated (he was met by the magistrates and the minister, who offered him the freedom 'if I could have staid', and they had a tavern bill of £1 17s. nevertheless); nine years later the Welsh traveller and naturalist Thomas Pennant found it 'distinguished for nothing but its large square tower, decorated with five small spires', but it was August fair-time and he found it gay with a show of hardware, printed linens and gay ribands. There is at least a hint that golf was being played at Tain by 1777, and about the time of Waterloo horse races were occasionally held on the links below the town or on the Morrich More.

The burgh boasted of only one wheeled carriage when a tax was imposed in 1785/86 — a four-wheeler with two horses belonging to Alexander Baillie of Knockbreck — but there were fifteen in the county as a whole. Lord Macleod, Balnagown, Geanies and Monro of Allan each had one, and the roads were being gradually improved as far as rather haphazard funds allowed. The burgh paid 6s. for snuff to the men 'at mending the King's Causeway' in 1732; part of the Edderton minister's stipend during a vacancy may have been applied towards repairing the road from Tain to Strathoykell in 1742; Balnagown asked for the assistance of soldiers to carry on the road from the water of Beauly to Dingwall and thence to Tain in 1764. Ross-shire had no turnpike roads at the beginning of the nineteenth century, and statute labour afforded the only means of repairing the highways. This was not popular, however, and eleven Tain apprentices — shoemakers, smiths, wrights, etc. — were reported to the justices of the peace as defaulters in 1802.

With the appointment of the Commissioners for Highland Roads and Bridges, under Telford's guiding genius as engineer, the system was greatly improved. Ross-shire presented some of their toughest problems, and the 'infinite mutability' of the lairds' intentions did not make them easier (Glastullich maintained that he was burdened with an extra 1,000 guineas for roads and bridges through a wrong decision by Geanies). In 1808 the first carrier went from Dingwall to Tain, and after the Conon was bridged in 1809 — the Beauly had to wait another five years — the journey from north of the Meikle Ferry to Edinburgh by the Inverness coach could be done within 48 hours. The old route was given an unenviable notoriety by the loss of 99 lives when the ferry-boat was swamped in 1809, and with the great high road built across the moor from Novar toll by Aultnamain and Struie to the new bridge at Bonar, some of the through traffic passed Tain by as it still does today.

A statutory road assessment, under which Tain paid £60 annually, was introduced in 1826, and when the question of Reform was agitating men's minds the anxiously-awaited news from the south was brought by a daily mail diligence which was drawn by four horses as far as Tain.

10

Tain church

WHEN Hugh Ross of Cromarty became the first provost after the reform of burgh administration in Scotland, Tain was noted for its irregularity of form even among the irregularly built towns of the North of Scotland. 'Every man', it was said, 'seems to have placed his house just as happened to suit his private convenience'.

There were by this time several new and handsome houses, built of the mellow fawn or honey-coloured sandstone quarried from the hill behind the town. But still, as older folk were to recall, more than one low-walled thatched house 'destroyed the look of our principal street and gave a mean and poverty-stricken appearance to the whole town'. The sidewalks were narrow and inconvenient, and the streets were paved with stones from the sea-shore; they may have been lit at night, for a lamplighter was employed by the council, but it was a year or so before they took over some of the Inverness street-lamps when that burgh changed to gas.

113

Only the newly-erected suburb to the south-east had any deliberately planned regularity, and the open stream named the Aultmaiteach was crossed by a bridge that was reckoned to be handsome.

Telford's great high road from north to south crossed the hills some miles to the west of Tain, but the post-road which still used the Meikle Ferry passed through the town. Every afternoon the mail coach left for Dornoch, Wick and Thurso, and every evening for Inverness. The roads were busy, too, for Tain was the county town of Ross, where the annual meetings of the freeholders and commissioners of supply were held; the seat of the presbytery of Tain and the synod of Ross; and the capital of an extensive district of farming country.

As befitted a place of this importance, it had a number of public buildings which gave it a special character. The old collegiate church was sadly neglected, and the parish church which took its place the year before Waterloo was still without a spire (as it was to remain); but the minister was thinking in terms of an additional church to provide for his large congregation, and the rumblings of the controversy which was to lead to a proliferation of churches were already being heard. The old steeple — the 'sharp-pointed house' as it was called — stood foursquare in the centre of the town; but the new jail and courthouse adjacent had been burnt out in 1833 after standing for only eight years; the outer walls were now a desolate mass of ruins, and the law courts met in the masonic hall. The new academy, barely twenty years old, was an embellishment to the town, which also boasted a grammar school, an English school, and — 'more unusual' — a boarding school for young ladies, all supported at least in part out of the burgh's common good. There was also 'a building for assemblies'; two inns, George Turnbull's Crown & Anchor and James Ellison's George & Dragon; and (if we are to believe some later recollections) a public-house in nearly every street, open all night and every day of the week.

Public services in the modern sense had not appeared, although the generation then living was to see many of them introduced, and there had been no effective collection of stent

114

since 1823. The inhabitants had to wait nearly seventy years more for a regular municipal water supply, but there was excellent drinking water in abundance. Nearly every household owned a well, but the water from that source, being brackish, was little used except for washing. In the old town there were four springs, the most famous of which was 'Donald Og's Well', and the people of the Newtown of Tain were supplied with drinking water from a fountain on Hartfield Road (until it was diverted to water the lands of Aldie). It was long remembered how each morning the housewives would assemble at a large well at the foot of Castle Brae, where a queue of from twenty to thirty water-carriers would be seen talking and gossiping as they waited their turn to draw water. The town still had no proper sanitation[1], and the drains were nearly all open, while the Aultmaiteach ran merrily below its bridge between the High Street and Lamington Street.

Tain was the biggest town north of Inverness, but its trade was still 'chiefly confined to domestic purposes' (according to a directory of the day), while its neighbour Invergordon, although only 'a respectable village', had its own harbour and two extensive hemp factories. There was, however, a great variety of occupations in Tain, which about this time gave employment to twenty drapers, seven wine merchants, six 'fleshers' or butchers, five joiners, four bakers, shoemakers, grocers and tailors, besides saddlers, cabinetmakers, cartwrights, ironmongers, watchmakers, a working silversmith, an earthenware dealer, and a turner in wood. There were also the minister and several school teachers, three surgeons and five 'writers' or lawyers, two bankers, and two innkeepers.

Besides providing for the needs of the townsman, of course, these people also served those in the villages and countryside around — in fact the whole of Easter Ross and part of Sutherland as well. On Tuesdays and Fridays there were markets 'well supplied with abundance of fish and butcher's meat', and at the time of the yearly fairs, some of which continued for several days, the streets were so crowded that it was almost

1   In the cholera epidemic of 1832 Tain had 55 deaths, and the fishing village of Inver lost 41 in a few days out of a population of between 120 and 140.

impossible to walk along them. Stalls stretched on either side of the High Street, from The Grove to the old churchyard, and even there the flat gravestones were used as tables.

At a time when a farm of 150 arable acres in the neighbourhood of Tain would be worked by three ploughmen and six day labourers, and even large farms did not usually employ boarded servants, hiring was obviously an important part of town life. When extra harvest hands were needed, the drummer went the rounds several times a day, crying 'Shearers wanted for —————; cairt to meet them at Sandy Munro the carrier's'. Strings of carts full of peats were driven into the town every morning (it was not uncommon to see a row of them from the present post-office to the town house), and those who were up earliest had choice of the best. Such fuel was plentiful, and there was coal to be had from Brora on the nearby coast of Sutherland.

Almost everyone in the town spoke English, and although there were some sixty or so with nothing but Gaelic the old tongue was rapidly losing ground. By then it was rare to find a townsman under twenty able to speak it with ease; it was almost unheard among the children on the streets. Old customs died slowly, however, and the New Year was still celebrated on the 12th of January. Superstition was common, and some people were supposed to have the second sight with its uncomfortable 'gift' of being able to foretell death and disaster. The Fendom road had the reputation of being haunted, and uncanny spectres — which no mere memory of a duel could account for — were constantly being seen there. Among cures for the sick the fresh spring water of St. Mary's Well — some threescore yards out from the shore to the west of the town, and covered twice daily by the sea — was reckoned a specific remedy for consumption, so long as the water was drunk early and on the spot.

Between the Tain of 1833 and the royal burgh of today there are many differences — some obvious physical changes which are there for all to see, and also some subtler undertones of experience, both in body and in spirit, which make the town and its people different from what they were. The picture would not be complete even in outline if some of these were not indicated.

The faults and failings which had brought about the demand for burgh reform were fully revealed by an exhaustive inquiry into the state of the municipal corporations of Scotland, ordered by the first reformed parliament at the same time that the method of election was changed. The general report of a special commission, published in 1835, referred to the alienation of property to members of the council in Tain, and also commented on the 'evident excess' in expenditure on civic entertainments. Among the commission's local reports, which enter into more detail, that on Tain (signed by Robert Hunter and Cosmo Innes) gives a useful summary of the revenue and expenditure of the burgh at this period.

Its heritable property consisted of arable land to the extent of about fifty acres, two mills and some houses, the superiority of an extensive tract of moorland, a mussel scalp on the shore of the Dornoch Firth[1], extensive seat-room in the church, and the jail and courthouse. The revenue from these, along with £37 13s. derived annually from customs and market dues, was £314; this was considerably exceeded by the expenditure of £495, which included £73 in salaries.

The commission had also been asked to recommend a new 'sett' for each burgh, to be determined mainly on a basis of population, and to define their boundaries. For Tain they proposed nine councillors, including a provost and two bailies — the same number for Dingwall, while Ross-shire's other royal burgh of Fortrose was to have six. Tain was considered to be in a thriving condition, and to allow for probable extension the commission proposed a boundary as follows:—

'From St. Mary's Well on the north-west of the town, in a straight line through the Ravens Well to a point 500 yards beyond the same; thence in a straight line, drawn due south-east, to the Scotsburn Road; thence in a straight line, drawn due east, to the Inverness Road; thence in a straight line drawn due north-east,

---

1 The report says that the scalps were not let, but fishermen paid for the mussels as they took them at a price of from 30s. to 40s. a boat-load.

to the River of Tain; thence down the River of Tain to the point at which the same joins the sea; thence along the sea shore to St. Mary's Well.'

As might be expected, it was not long before the old problem of the head burgh of Ross was revived, in relation to the place for holding the county meetings, and the new provost — also not unexpectedly — was in the forefront of the controversy. Noted even in those days for shortness of temper, he complained that Duncan Davidson of Tulloch had interrupted him in an uncalled-for manner at an Invergordon meeting, and there was a token duel between them in which neither was hurt. Not long after, at the beginning of a meeting in Dingwall, Ross handed in a protest against its legality and dramatically warned the assembled gentlemen that 'he would meet them again at Philippi'.

The issue was finally settled in August 1843, when an 'Act for appointing the Royal Burgh of Dingwall to be the Head Burgh of the Shire of Ross' (6 & 7 Vict. cap. 92) was passed through both Houses of Parliament. Dingwall celebrated its victory with rejoicing, and gave the freedom to two of the Bill's supporters; not to be outdone, Tain added three new freemen to its roll — James Matheson of Achany, who had been most liberal to the academy and soon afterwards succeeded Hugh Ross of Cromarty as chairman of directors; Sir William C. Ross, a distinguished artist whose grandfather was a native of the burgh; and young Lieutenant Robert Bruce Æneas Macleod of Cadboll, in recognition of his gallant conduct as a naval officer in Syria and elsewhere, and as a mark of the town's respect for his father and aged grandfather (the trouble-making Roderick of one generation earlier being conveniently forgotten).

But the year was chiefly memorable for the Disruption out of which the Free Church was born. The restoration of church patronage still rankled, but the real issue in the 'ten years' conflict' which reached its crisis in 1843 was the doctrine of spiritual independence — the proper relation between church and state, linked as it was bound to be in a period of democratic progress with that of the individual and the community.

It was a controversy in which the Highlands generally, and perhaps Easter Ross in particular (with its Covenanting tradition), were keenly involved. There was an intensity of feeling on all religious issues which is not easily appreciated today — Dr Duff, pioneer of Indian missions, spoke for two and a half hours from the pulpit of the church of Tain in 1835, and four years later Dr Chalmers had a full audience of upwards of a thousand for an address on church extension ('a marvellous day meeting in so small a place', he noted — 'much pleased with the antique and simple air of the town of Tain'). The population of the parish, Gaelic and English, was near its peak, and the church so inadequate that the minister (Charles Calder Mackintosh, who had succeeded his father) talked of having the abandoned collegiate church repaired and brought back into use[1].

The decade of conflict opened with the General Assembly declaring it a fundamntal law of the Church of Scotland that no pastor should be 'intruded' on any congregation contrary to the will of the people. The parish and presbytery — with Mackintosh as moderator — were soon caught up in the tide of national events: when the Court of Session (later upheld by the House of Lords) declared the Assembly's 'veto act' illegal, they declared the independence of the church in doctrine, worship and discipline against all interference by the civil courts, and later voted their sympathy and approval to a presbytery which had been rebuked for breach of interdict.

In February 1840 a meeting in support of 'non-intrusion' was held in Tain, and in April the presbytery adopted a petition on the subject for transmission to both Houses of Parliament. Feeling was running high, and Provost Ross resigned in protest when the town council elected a non-intrusion commissioner from the burgh to the General Assembly, after urging without success that he should be instructed to oppose any measure aimed at defeating the decisions of the civil courts. In a pamphlet giving his reasons he defended the system of patronage, pointed out that all the ministers who had

1 Certain of the parishioners hived off in 1838 because of the enormous seat-rents in the new parish church and built their own chapel in Cadboll Place, with seating for 300.

attended the Tain meeting had been presented by the patrons in accordance with the wishes of the people, and declared that opposition to patronage was particularly uncalled for in Tain, where 'for the last two hundred years the parishioners were consulted on the appointment of their minister'.

When the crisis came, all the ministers of the presbytery severed their connection with the established church, except the dying Hugh Ross of Fearn, and the only elder left was old Macleod of Cadboll. Although he lost his church, manse and stipend, Mackintosh of Tain used to say that he 'walked on air' on the Disruption day, and his congregation and practically the entire population joined him in seceding. In the wooden Free Church building which was erected within a few weeks, the magistrates took their places opposite the pulpit as they had previously done in the established church, and they continued to do so — walking in procession behind their red-coated halbert-armed officers — until a hint from Edinburgh that it was of questionable legality (the same thing had been done in Kirkcaldy) reduced it to a personal and unofficial demonstration. Another sign of solidarity came during two summer communions after the Disruption, when the Free Church pitched a tent for the Gaelic congregation in the old churchyard, as used to be done before 1815, and between two and three thousand people gathered; a sheriff's interdict was served on them, but 'the whole town turned out as one man' and transferred the tent, table, forms and chairs to a field near the Free Church.

Although sadly depleted, the established church struggled to fill the vacant parishes. Lewis Rose, who had already been minister of Nigg and Kincardine in the same presbytery, was called to Tain in 1844 and ministered there for another 32 years. Previously, while minister of Duke Street Gaelic Church in Glasgow, he had published 'an address to the ministers and people of Scotland' in an attempt to put an end to the divisions in the church. It showed his familiarity with acts of assembly and of parliament and other official documents, although he is said to have been one of forty ministers expected to 'come out' in 1843 who at the last moment decided to stay in the establishment. In spite of sectarian divisions and bitterness, Rose visited all homes where trouble was, irrespective of denomination, and one who remembered him wrote long afterwards: 'His face was a sermon and his smile a benediction'.

On the Free Church side, Mackintosh was translated to Dunoon in 1854, but he left a congregation strong enough not to be seriously affected by a four-year vacancy. For his successor, Thomas Grant, Tain was his only charge during a ministry which extended over 48 years. He was a man of strong character whose services were 'eagerly sought and greatly prized' all over the Highlands.

Meantime, for a generation, the old collegiate church had been left uncared for, a prey to vandalism and decay. Catherine Sinclair was 'quite scandalized' to see it so disreputable — pews torn up by the roots, galleries hanging in splinters, curtains in tatters, the windows broken and partly built up, the tombs defaced, the pulpit stair a wreck, and the desk 'tottering towards the ground'. In 1848, after a further eight years of neglect, the hymn-writer John Mason Neale, who as an ecclesiologist appreciated the details of its architecture, was equally depressed — 'the dampness, the rottenness, the horrible filth, the green mould, the decaying baize, the deserted appearance of the whole, render this a shocking place', he wrote.

Yet it was not until 1857 that a number of people whose relatives and friends were buried in the church or the adjacent churchyard sought and obtained permission from the heritors to carry out repairs. A subscription was set on foot, and a committee appointed, and by the end of 1859 Provost John M'Leod was able to launch an appeal not only to friends in Tain and the neighbourhood, but also to natives and former residents scattered throughout the world. The churchyard was tidied up and enclosed, and the roof reslated as a first step towards preservation, and it was soon obvious that funds would be sufficient to renovate the fabric within and without so as to make it an object of architectural interest. The next stage was to open the original entrances, and remove the galleries and seats on the ground floor, as well as the rubble-work which destroyed the effect of the fine east window and others. By 1870 the roof and walls had been completely repaired, and the stonework of some of the windows renewed.

It was agreed that the building should not again be used as a regular place of worship, but should be dedicated to monumental purposes as 'the Valhalla of Ross-shire'. The restoration of the stonework was completed through the generosity of Alexander Brodie Mackintosh, grandson of the last minister; Kenneth Murray of Geanies, Sheriff Harry Munro Taylor, Hugh Law Rose of Tarlogie, and the provost's son George M'Leod, late of Bengal. The windows were filled with stained glass by James Ballantine & Son of Edinburgh.

The whole work was carried out under the supervision of Robert Matheson, head of the Board of Works in Scotland, himself a native of Tain and an architect of ability. The total cost was about £650, and in 1876 Provost M'Leod and Sheriff Taylor arranged, as sole survivors of the Guildry Society of Tain, that its funds should be transferred to trustees for the future maintenance of the church and churchyard. Special appeals later raised enough to restore the Regent Moray pulpit (using recovered fragments of the original ornamentation of which it had been almost entirely stripped, and Matheson's recollection of its appearance when he was a boy), and for monuments to Thomas Hog of Kiltearn and the martyr Patrick Hamilton.

Since then the collegiate church of St. Duthac may be said to have been in dignified retirement, except for a few special occasions, while its work was carried on by a variety of successors. A building of the 'Disruption type' with accommodation for 1,500 soon replaced the wooden church, and the Free Church congregation played a dominant part in the life of the town. The American evangelists, Moody and Sankey, visited the church in 1874, leaving a deep impression on those who heard them, and in the same year patronage was abolished. In 1891/2 a new building designed by a local firm of architects, Andrew Maitland & Sons, was erected; as a result of the Free Church union with the United Presbyterian Church to form the United Free Church in 1900, and the U.F. Church union with the Church of Scotland in 1929, followed by a local union of congregations in 1942, this church now serves the great majority of families in the parish. Its 107-foot spire makes it a prominent landmark, and inside it has been enhanced in recent years by fine stained glass windows, one of them in memory of Sir John Fraser, the surgeon and principal of Edinburgh University, by Douglas Hamilton, R.S.A.

The former parish church, in which the first pipe organ introduced in the North had been installed in 1905, was sold to the town council in 1946 and is now used as a town hall. There is a Free Church in Scotsburn Road, built in 1938, and an Episcopal Church in Manse Street dating from 1887, both of which succeeded temporary 'iron churches'.

Tain owes much of its charm as a town to the fact that many of its houses are of native stone from the Tain quarries. This has been used in a number of public buildings, although the persistent tradition that it was second on the selection list for the Houses of Parliament in 1840 is not borne out by the parliamentary records of the day. The Victorian era saw the rise of many of Tain's own institutions, as well as the restoration of her chief architectural gem, and for a small town they have a startling variety of style and purpose.

The foundation stone of a new courthouse and council chamber, 'a handsome pinnacled edifice in the Scottish baronial style' on the site of the building burnt down, was laid in September 1848, and additions made in 1873; the first poorhouse built in the Highlands, for the nine parishes of Easter Ross, was opened in 1850, and now fulfils a contemporary role as 'Arthurville'; a public hall to accommodate nearly 600, French Renaissance in style, was built in 1875-76 between the new Royal Hotel and Tower Gardens, and reopened as a town hall in August 1903 after being repainted and redecorated at Andrew Carnegie's expense; a clock with three dials was added to the old steeple in 1877, under a bequest by Frederick Campbell Taylor, merchant (replacing an older one-faced clock made in Tain about 1750); in 1879 a monument in Decorated Gothic style was erected to the memory of Kenneth Murray of Geanies, with a marble bust under the central arch by T. S. Burnett, a young Edinburgh sculptor; an ornamental gateway leading into the churchyard was provided in 1885 in memory of William Ross, bank agent; the market cross was restored in 1895 on the original base, with a new top and restored shaft, at the expense of Dr James Vass, a former provost; a public shambles was built 'in the Lombardic style' in 1885; a new masonic hall for St. Duthus Lodge was opened in Queen Street in 1895; and the tradesmen of the town gave their spare-time services free to build a hall for the Oddfellows Friendly Society. Andrew Carnegie, who was made a freeman in 1899, presented a free library to the town which was opened in 1904.

The academy's progress was halted more than once by shortage of funds and other difficulties, causing reductions in staff and even temporary closure, and appeals to the public in 1841, 1843 and 1858. The rector from 1850-54 was Professor Peter Wilson, who once held the same post in Inverness Royal Academy, and acquired his title by having filled the chair of natural philosophy in the Andersonian College in Glasgow. After his death the academy had a remarkable succession of four rectors whose reigns covered a total of 110 years — John Scott (1854-87), Andrew Harris Hutt (1887-1919), Andrew Mackie (1919-45) and Robert Hay (1945-64) — and who raised it to a high position among the schools of Scotland.

A report published as a prelude to the Education Act of 1872 gives a glimpse of teaching at the academy a century ago. With about 100 scholars on the roll — three-quarters of them boys, one-quarter girls — it was reckoned that the total cost of a full ten-year course was £37. The parents were mostly clergymen, farmers, merchants, and 'the more comfortable class of master tradesman', and they could choose which courses they wished their children to follow. Tain was then the only burgh in Scotland in which there was a demand for Italian to be taught, along with the customary French and German, English and classical tongues. The burgh still contributed only £25 to the academy out of an annual revenue (for 1855/6) of £902, and the reporters asked: 'If the Tain community demands such variety of instruction, could it not provide funds to pay more instructors?'

In 1888 a new administrative scheme brought into the academy's governing body a number of elected representatives of the community as well as of the subscribers; from 1912 its management came under the local school board; and since the passing of another Education Act in 1918 — sometimes known as the 'Munro Act', because it was introduced by the M.P. for the Northern Burghs as Secretary for Scotland — the academy has been administered by the county education authority.

The Established and Free Church schools were united in 1873 under Peter Bain, poet, artist, orator, 'a man of great culture and of strikingly handsome appearance'. It continued as Tain public school in the building at the east end of the town, was practically doubled in size in 1909, and finally united with the academy in 1937.

As education became standardised, there was a tendency for people also to conform to a pattern, even in the remoter parts of the country. Donald Macleod of Geanies had died in 1834, after sixty years as sheriff, Hugh Ross of Cromarty followed in 1846, and although the Murray family provided a number of provosts and benefactors to Tain the rugged personalities became fewer. Perhaps it was partly, as must always happen, that some of the more enterprising characters found their life's work elsewhere, far from the streets of Tain: although one of them used to recall that even in the heart of London he felt a sense of homeliness and importance from the knowledge that the sheep which browsed in Hyde Park or St. James's came from the parishes of Tarbat and Fearn, as the grazings in the royal parks were rented by an Easter Ross family.

One local personality who bridged the years in an exceptional way was Bailie Alexander Wallace, church elder, freemason, volunteer, and supporter of every charitable organisation. Born in Rosskeen parish in 1813, he came to Tain about 1830 and was 'almost a native' when he died in 1911. He went into the Free Church with Angus MacIntosh at the Disruption, and took part in the induction of a successor 68 years later, and it was said of him that 'although he carries the years of a patriarch and the reputation of a saint, he has the spirits of a schoolboy'. His portrait by Fiddes Watt, presented on his 95th birthday, still hangs in the council chamber where he sat for 42 years as a councillor and 32 as a magistrate.

Politics had come to play a less active part in the life of Tain, although there were times when controversy rose high over local, national or even international issues. James Loch lost the Northern Burghs to an independent Liberal, Samuel Laing, in 1852, and the long reign of John Pender from 1872 to 1896 (broken by an interval of seven years when the seat was held by J. Macdonald Cameron) was followed by T. C. H. Hedderwick, Sir Arthur Bignold, and Robert Munro (later Lord Alness), who was Secretary for Scotland when the Northern Burghs ceased to be a separate constituency in 1918, and the electorate of Tain was included in Ross and Cromarty.

Like most small and closely-knit communities, especially before the advent of the cinema, radio and television, Tain supported a multitude of societies which had a social as well as a cultural and eduational value. Among them were the Tain Literary Society, founded in 1870, which enjoyed many outstanding speakers and debates, and the Tain Musical Society, which presented a series of Gilbert and Sullivan operas beginning with 'The Gondoliers' in 1913. In later years, despite competing interests, the burgh became a stronghold of the community drama movement.

The railway reached Tain in 1864, revolutionising travel and transport, and incidentally cutting through the Angel Hill and giving passengers the best of all views of the town, with its striking outline of church and steeple against the sky. This brought more visitors to the North, the first members of the royal family to make the journey by rail being the Prince and Princess of Wales (later Edward VII and Queen Alexandra) on their way to Dunrobin in 1866, followed by the Queen herself in 1872. When he had such special guests, the Duke of Sutherland used to meet them at Inverness with his own engine and saloon carriage, and drive them the rest of the journey himself. The railway train in turn has yielded its supremacy to the motor-car, which first appeared in Tain about 1908, and buses now link the town with others to the north and south.

Towards the end of the nineteenth century a small fleet of

coastal schooners used to ply their trade from Tain, bringing from the Baltic sawn timber which was used in some of the public buildings and large houses of the town. As Tain has no harbour of its own, these ships came in at high water, and when the tide ebbed carts went out to collect their cargo. One of them, the St. Duthus (79 tons), was lost in collision with a Hull steam trawler about 100 miles off Spurn Head while on a voyage from London to Inverness in February 1903, when she was 28 years old; the crew of five and one passenger were saved. Less fortunate were the three men on a 35-ton iron steamship, the Sterlina of Glasgow, which was driven on the Gizzen Briggs while trying to make her way out of the Dornoch Firth with a strong breeze from the east and a heavy sea running in December 1910; she was soon submerged in quicksands, leaving only a portion of the mast above water, and during the night two of the crew succumbed to the intense cold within sight of the lights of Tain; the third was rescued by the Portmahomack pilot boat in an exhausted condition after close on twenty hours in the rigging.

The fishing industry having extended with the construction of railways far more rapidly than the natural increase of bait supplies, the town's mussel scalps became a very lucrative property, and the drawings reached a peak of £1,085 15s. in 1879/80. At that period nearly all the 50,000 fishermen of Scotland used mussels as their bait during at least some part of the year, and for ordinary white fish such as haddock, whiting and cod the mussel stood alone as bait. When it is realised that a single boat might use as much as 38 tons of mussels in a year, costing £66, and that the weight of mussels used might be little less than the weight of fish caught, it is plain that a burgh owning scalps where some of the best mussels in Scotland grew, with undisputed charter rights dating back to the seventeenth century, had a valuable asset with which to build up its common good.

No record was kept of the quantity sold from the town scalps of Tain, but a table of income and expenditure from 1856 to 1888 was included in evidence before a parliamentary committee which was appointed as a result of complaints from fishermen about the growing scarcity and rising price of mussels[1]. The inquiry covered the whole of Scotland, and the committee held its first meeting in the courthouse of Tain in October 1888, when Provost Vass, two members of the town council's 'mussel committee', and the manager of the town scalps (Captain Elder) were examined. An extract of Charles II's charter of 1671 was handed in by the provost, and it was explained that the principal scalp, called the Black Scalp, was about 300 yards long and its average breadth about 120 yards; the Red Scalp not more than 60 or 70 yards long by about 50 yards broad; and the inshore scalps, scattered over a part of the beach about three-quarters of a mile long and 100 to 150 yards broad, with large portions where there were no scalps.

The evidence gives full details of how the beds were conducted and some attempts made to improve them. The committee found that the Scottish mussel fisheries generally were conducted in a 'most wasteful, improvident and uneconomic manner', the chief consideration being how to supply the wants of the moment without thought for the future, and there can be little doubt that they were justified in including the mussel beds of Tain among those which, with great natural advantages, had been 'abused and neglected'.

Although Tain has never been an industrial town, a number of private enterprises have been carried on in or near it. These include the Glenmorangie Distillery (founded in 1843), a brewery, foundry[2], bacon factory, coach works, wool and meal mills, and laundry. The first and last of these are still operating, and a recently-founded business produces a cream cheese and 'crowdie' which have made the name of Tain familiar even among those who have not visited it.

1   Although in some years very large sales were effected, in 1884/5 the income was £8 10s. and in 1885/6 there was no income whatever; in 1887/8, owing to a slight improvement of the beds, probably proceeding from attempts made to grow mussels on the bed system, the income was £77 5s. Expenditure on the Tain beds never exceeded £124, and apart from a few peak years it was generally under £50, in striking contrast to the Duke of Sutherland's Little Ferry beds at Loch Fleet, where annually over £200 and in one year over £500 was spent. (*Report of the Committee on the Scottish Mussel and Bait Beds*, 1889; chairman, Edward Marjoribanks, M.P.) Because of the decline of the Scottish small-line fishery, which has largely been replaced by seine-netting and other methods, the demand for mussels in Scotland has almost vanished, and the Tain scalps are now let for £5 per annum.
2   The foundry, which operated at the west end of the town, and was described as 'very dilapidated' in 1870, was owned by a family called Ferguson, and wrought mainly in brass. One of the family invented a swing plough called after him, which was widely used throughout the North and won prizes at ploughing matches for its users. (Information from the Rev. R. W. A. Begg, compiler of the Third Statistical Account of Tain.)

Tain has long been popular as a holiday resort, for which it has many claims to favour. Cricket is one of its longest-established sports, traditionally dating back to an English butler, Walter Crouch, who was in service with a local family in the 1860s. He introduced the game to Ross-shire and arranged friendly matches with players in neighbouring towns and villages. At one time four separate teams found support in the burgh, largely through the zeal of an Australian, Harry Cullington, who was employed by a local firm of meal millers. The St. Duthus Cricket Club, when already a veteran of about seventy years, entered the North of Scotland competitive lists in 1946, and visitors from the south have been amazed to find play continuing on the Links up to 10.30 p.m. in the long daylight of a northern summer.

Tain Golf Club was instituted in 1890 as a result of the enthusiasm of Alexander Macbean, who learnt his golf at St. Andrews, and while in India was one of the founders of the Lucknow club. On coming to Tain he saw the possibilities of the sandy links by the seaside, where nature would provide the hazards for a first-class course. Tom Morris laid it out, and Willie Auchterlonie pronounced it the most varied and testing that he knew. As the number of summer visitors increased, the course was reorganised and extended and a new clubhouse opened in 1911. When the fleet was in the Cromarty Firth there was a constant stream of naval guests, and the course had become the principal asset of the town in attracting visitors by August 1914, when 'despite war's alarms' the town council purchased the Kirksheaf estate — including the old farm of 'Kirkscaith' and the historic Plaids — to enable further improvements to be made.

Lawn tennis, bowling, duck shooting, loch and burn fishing, and sea bathing were listed among the other attractions of Tain as a holiday resort at the beginning of the century, and its climate and situation were extolled. In a list of local societies in 1907 were numbered the golf and cricket clubs, a lawn tennis club, football club, hockey club, clay pigeon club, bowling club, and curling club, some of which survive.

Two world wars left their mark on the burgh, as they did on

all others throughout the country, and 122 names of those who died in the first war and 27 in the second are inscribed on memorial tablets in Tain's 'Valhalla'. The burgh had a long record of support for the county regiment, the Seaforth Highlanders (now amalgamated with a sister regiment to form the Queen's Own Highlanders), and on at least one occasion when volunteers were being raised for home defence the Tain company was the first enrolled north of the Spey. Territorial Army camps on the Morrich Mor are still remembered by some old soldiers, but that desolate expanse of moor and marsh with its offshore islands was sold by the burgh to the Air Ministry and is used as a bombing range. After the second war the lands of Culpleasant and Lairg were sold for use by the Forestry Commission; the sale included the Tain quarries, reopened in 1952/53 after having been closed since 1915; the stone was used for restoration work in Stirling, and for the North of Scotland Hydro-Electric Board's power stations at Torr Achilty and Moss Ford in the Conon valley.

Except when the winter snows block the hill road over Struie, most of the heavy traffic moving between north and south passes Tain by. But the old burgh is the business and shopping centre of a wide and active agricultural area, and it is within easy reach of the coastal fringe and hills of Easter Ross which are making an increasing appeal to tourists and summer visitors. Ambitious plans are now being discussed for modern industrial development in the region round the firths towards Inverness, and if this materialises Tain might find itself much sought after as providing congenial surroundings for those who work elsewhere in the neighbourhood. The burgh has set apart a modest area beside the Shore Road as a site for light industry; new and attractive post-war housing is a feature of the town; and after many disheartening delays the ground has now been broken between Scotsburn Road and Hartfield Road for the building which is to replace the original Tain Royal Academy — 'looking perhaps a trifle tired after its 150 years' — and provide a fine new school for future generations.

But in the midst of change, Tain has retained the dignity

which comes with the years and the centuries. When Her Majesty the Queen and His Royal Highness the Duke of Edinburgh made a brief visit to the burgh on Thursday, 25th June 1964, they 'lichtit' at the ancient market cross, which was on record in the sixteenth century; the town's bellman rang the old Flemish bell dating from 1630 to mark their arrival; and in the council chamber, they were shown the charter of James VI confirming the privileges of the burgh in 1588, the bull of Pope Innocent VIII recognising the collegiate church in 1492 (in a silver frame presented by Andrew Carnegie), and the notarial copy of the inquest of 1439 relating that the immunity of Tain was founded by Her Majesty's ancestor Malcolm Canmore.

Today two royal portraits, signed 'Elizabeth' and 'Philip', hang on the wall of the chamber, with the burgh arms depicting St. Duthac between them. There, as in the pages of this book, Tain's nine hundred years of history are written.

The new Academy (projected)

Provosts of Tain from 1833

1833–1840	Hugh Rose Ross of Cromarty
1840–1848	George Murray of Rosemount
1848–1857	William H. Murray of Geanies
1858–1875	John Macleod
1876–1890	James Vass
1890–1897	Edward H. McK. Matheson
1879–1898	Andrew Maitland
1898–1910	Donald Fowler
1910–1921	James Maitland
1921–1924	James Robertson
1924–1930	William Ross
1930–1933	William J. Munro
1933–1936	Donald Ross
1936–1945	William Fraser
1945–1949	David Geekie
1949–1954	John Fletcher
1954–1958	A. W. Macdonald
1958–1964	A. G. D. Cameron
1964–	Robert Hay

Ross-shire Burgh Populations

Year	Dingwall	Fortrose	Invergordon	Tain
1841	1739	1082	998	2287
1851	1990	1148	—	2588
1861	2099	928	1122	2319
1871	2125	1007	1157	2287
1881	1932	991	1119	2221
1891	2300	980	1117	2084
1901	2519	1179	1047	2076
1911	2639	970	1051	1599
1921	2323	963	1384	1551
1931	2553	875	1417	1383
1941	—	—	—	—
1951	3367	882	1514	1600
1961	3752	903	1642	1699

INDEX

(see also lists on pages 35, 38, 39 and 132)

134

136

streets 71, 80, 86, 113
superstitions 116
tolbooth (steeple) 54, 73, 74, 80, 84, 108n, 114
town bell 54, 72, 131
town clerks 53, 72, 91 (and see D. and J. Forrester, W. Fraser, C. Manson, D. Ross, A. Taylor)
town clock 72, 123
town council 71, 75, 76, 80, 89, 103
town hall (later cinema) 123; (former church) 123
trade 12, 35, 36, 42, 52, 53, 70, 72, 79
vicarage 19, 22, 25, 30
war memorial 130
Washing Burn 72
water supply 88, 115
wells 106, 115, 116, 117
Tain, Hill of 6, 21, 74; Little 106; Newtown of 114, 115; river 6, 118
Tain plantation (Berbice) 109
Tantallon castle 19, 44
Tarbat Ness 6; parish 7, 8, 21, 63, 101, 125; Viscount (see Cromartie)
Tarlogie 25, 89, 106; chaplainry 26, 33
Tarrel, Andrew 35n; William 35n
Taylor, Alexander 98; Frederick C. 123; Harry Munro 122
Telford, Thomas 112, 114
Thomson, Patrick 110
Thorfinn, Earl 9, 11, 12

Thornton, John 31
Thurlow, Lord Chancellor 95
Thurso 72, 114
Torr Achilty power station 130
Torrannabuachil 88
Torvadroy 88
Transatlantic Association 108
Tucker, Thomas 70
Turnbull, George 114
Ulladill: see Scotsburn
Union, Cromwellian 61, 62; Act of (1707) 75, 76
Urquhart of Cromarty, Sir Thomas 64
Usurpation 74
Vass of Lochslin, John 38, 45, 46
Vass, Dr James 124, 128
Victoria, queen 126
Wallace, Alexander 125
Watt, Fiddes 125
Whitehills 81
Whithorn 28, 30, 54
Wick 38, 41, 42, 72, 75, 96, 114
Wilkie, R. M. 110
William the Lion 15, 36; III 68, 69, 71
Williamson, Angus 54
Wilson, Peter 52, 124
Witchcraft 45, 48
Wolseley, Robert 62
Worcester, battle of 57, 61
Wyvis, Ben 6

138